Summer Fit Activities™

Third to Fourth Grade

Build Fit Brains and Fit Bodies!

 Fun, skill based activities in reading, writing, mathematics, and language arts with additional activities in science and geography. Curriculum activities are based on national standards.

 Summer Fitness program includes aerobic and strength exercises.. Fitness log, exercise videos and instructions included. Keeping young bodies active and strong helps children live better, learn more and feel healthier.

 Incentive Contract Calendars motivate children to complete activities and exercises by rewarding their efforts. Summer Explorers are lists of fun and active things to do — perfect for when your child says, "I'm bored, what can I do?"

 Core values and role model activities include child activities, parent talking points and reading lists.

 Summer Journaling, Book Reports, Health and Nutrition Index, Certificate of Completion and Flashcards.

D1304101

Access more summer resource materials at
www.SummerFitActivities.com

Written by: Kelly Terrill and Sarria James

Fitness and Nutrition: Lisa Roberts RN, BSN, PHN, Coach James Cordova and Charles Miller

Cover Illustration: Amanda Sorensen

Illustrations: Roxanne Ottley, Amanda Sorensen, Fernando Becerra, Richard Casillas, Jason Gould, Bess Li, Sarah Shah

Page Layout: Robyn Pettit

Special Thanks: Wildlife SOS

For orders or product information call 801-466-4272

Dedication

Summer Fit™ is dedicated to Julia Hobbs and Carla Fisher who are the original authors of Summer Bridge Activities™. Julia and Carla helped pioneer summer learning and dedicated their lives to their vocation of teaching.

Caution

Exercises may require adult supervision. If you have any concerns regarding your child's ability to complete any of the suggested fitness activities, consult your family doctor or pediatrician. Children should always stretch and warm up before exercises. Do not push children past comfort level or ability. Exercises were created to be fun for parents and caregivers as well as the child, but not as a professional training or weight loss program. Exercise should stop immediately if you or your child experiences any of the following symptoms: pain, feeling dizzy or faint, nausea, or severe fatigue.

Copyright

ISBN 978-0-9982902-4-9

SummerFitActivities.com

Table of Contents

Parent Section

Activities and Exercises

Section 1

Section 2

Section 3

Section 4

Section 5

Extras

★ = Academic   ● = Core Value   ▲ = Fitness   ■ = Writing   ◈ = Play & Do   ◆ = Track

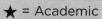

Dear Parent,

As a mother, I value giving my children the academic resources they need for success in both their personal and school life. However, when summer comes it is hard to resist the urge to shutter the books and toss the backpacks in the closet.

I have learned first hand that the lack of study over the summer holiday can cause summer learning loss. Studies show that as much as 2.5 months of learning can be undone and some children have lower test scores during the period directly after summer. It is important to find a balance between summer vacation and homework. **Summer Fit Activities** is the resource that does it while looking and feeling like academic summer camp.

Summer Fit Activities is an engaging workbook that helps your child learn and grow. It contains three different foundation pieces for your child's success: academics, health, and values that help children become kinder, more empathetic and stronger leaders. **Summer Fit Activities** makes learning fun with colorful illustrations, family activities, fitness logs, and incentive calendars. Summer Fit is easy to use for parents, caregivers and even grandparents, because day-by-day lesson plans are straightforward and flexible to allow you to create a summer learning experience specifically for your child.

Summer Fit Activities educates the whole child just like you would in summer camp- with an emphasis on FUN. My children love the healthy snack ideas they can make on their own and the Summer Explorer lists of outdoor learning activities that provide hands on learning experiences. I love the flashcards included in the back of book to help reinforce basic skills and the peace of mind knowing that I am teaching my child to be a great person, as well as a great student.

Summer is a time for adventure and fun, but it is also a time of learning and growth. With **Summer Fit Activities** I found the balance I was looking for - unplug, learn and let the magic of summer unfold before your eyes!

Have a wonderful summer,

Christa
Parent

INSIDE

Summer Fit Activities™

Here is what you will find inside Summer Fit™:

Academics

- There are 5 sections of academic exercises, each section with its own core value and journal entry page.

- Sections begin with Incentive Contract Calendars and "Summer Fitness Logs."

- Your child will complete activities in reading, writing, math and language arts. Science and geography activities are included throughout the book.

- When your child completes each day, he/she may color or initial the academic and reading icon for that day on the Incentive Contract Calendar.

- Parents initial the Incentive Contract Calendar once the section has been completed.

Fitness

Research shows that keeping bodies strong and healthy helps children learn better, live better and even miss fewer days of school! To keep bodies healthy, children need to eat right, get enough sleep and exercise daily.

- The Summer Fitness Program helps children set goals and track performance over the summer.

- Daily aerobic and strength exercises

- Fitness & Health Index includes Nutrition page, Foods to Eat Everyday & Meal Tracker.

- Online videos show the proper way to complete exercises.

Values Education

Core values are fundamental to society and are incorporated into our civil laws. Research shows that character education is more effective when parents encourage values in their child's daily routine. Core values are vitally important to the overall growth, well-being and success of all children.

- Each section highlights two different values and role models.

- Value activities are designed for children and parents.

- Each value includes a reading comprehension activity based on role models from throughout the world.

Helpful Hints for Summer Fit™

 Flip through the book to become familiar with the layout and activities. Look ahead to the upcoming core value so you can incorporate discussions and activities into your daily routine.

 Provide your child with the tools he/she will need to complete the work: pencils, pens, crayons, ruler, and healthy dose of encouragement.

 Try to set aside a specific time to do Summer Fit™ each day (for example, after breakfast each morning). Make sure your child has enough time to complete the day's work and exercise.

 Be a cheerleader! Encourage your child to do their best, urging them to challenge themselves. Make sure they know you are there to help them if they need support. Talk about and reinforce the material in the book beyond the page. For example, after reading about insects, encourage your child to find an insect in the yard to observe and draw.

 Look at your child's work frequently. Make sure they know you value what they are doing and it is not just "busywork".

 Try doing Summer Fit™ outside in the fresh air: at the park, in the backyard, camping, or on the beach. Summer Fit™ can go wherever you go!

 Ask older siblings, grandparents, babysitters and even friends to participate in and give one on one help with the activities. Summer Fit™ is great shared experience!

 Keep up with the Incentive Contract Calendars. Follow through and reward completed work: stamps, stickers, hugs, and high fives are great ways to motivate and recognize a job well done.

 Let your child do more than one page at a sitting if he/she is enthusiastic and wants to work ahead. Make sure to check the website for additional activities and resources that can help you tailor Summer Fit™ to your child's needs.

 When the book has been completed, display the Certificate of Completion proudly and let your child know what a great job he/she did. Celebrate!

Encourage Summer Reading and Writing

Reading and writing skills are important skills for your child's success. Summer is a great time to encourage and build reading and writing skills with your child regardless of ability.

You can do many things to encourage literacy and writing:

 Make Reading a Priority: Create a routine by establishing a reading time each day for your child.

 Read Around Your Child: Read in front of him/her as much as possible. Talk with your child about the books you are reading.

 Create a Summer Reading List: Find books that involve your child's favorite interests like sports, art, mysteries, dance, etc.

 Reading On The Road: Billboards, menus, street signs, window banners and packaging labels are great ways to reinforce reading comprehension skills.

 Storytelling: Have campfire nights in your backyard and tell stories about things you did when you were their age. Slip in a few scary spooks as well!

 Read Together: Newspapers, magazine articles and stories on the Internet are great to read together and discuss.

 Library Time: Go to the library on a weekly basis to choose new books.

 Letter Writing: Encourage your child to write thank you notes and letters.

 Plan a Trip: Have your child plan a trip for the family. Have him/her write an overview of the trip including where, what to bring, how to travel, how long and what you will do on your trip.

 Create a Joke Book: Provide a list of subjects for your child to create jokes about.

 Family Writing Hour: Sit down as a family and write a story together. Read the story out loud at the end.

Script Writing: Ask your child to write a movie script. When it is finished, perform it as a family – be sure to video the production!

Poetry: Discuss different forms of poetry. Have your child write a poem. Add an illustration.

Mindfulness

As a parent or guardian it is easy to get pulled into the many distractions of daily life. Have you ever wondered if your child has the same difficulties juggling personal interests with school with all the beeps, phone calls and text messages along the way?

Multitasking, compounded with technology, can make it difficult for all of us to concentrate on what we are doing in the moment. Growing research shows that we are hard wired to focus on one thing at a time. Teaching your child to be mindful and to focus on their internal feelings allows your child to fully experience what they are doing in the moment and can have a lasting effect on what, how and why they learn. Learning to sit without distractions and to focus on the moment is a gradual process that has immense benefits for you and your child.

Parent Tips to Help Children Be Mindful

 Time Set a time when all noises, distractions and devices are turned off — start with 5 minutes a day.

 Talk Ask your child to clear her thoughts and to focus on not thinking about anything.

 Focus Focus on breathing, take deep breathes and exhale slowly.

 Quiet Sit in silence.

 Show Show your child gratitude by thanking her for her time. Ask her what she is thankful for and discuss the importance of being grateful.

3-4 • © Summer Fit Activities™

Living Earth Friendly

We all share this home called Earth, and each one of us needs to be responsible in helping take care of her. There are many things families can do together to REDUCE, REUSE, and RECYCLE in order to be kind to Mother Earth. We can all BE SMART AND DO OUR PART!

There are many opportunities each day for us to practice these little steps with our children and we should talk with them about how little things add up to make a big impact.

REDUCE, REUSE, RECYCLE

REDUCE: Means to use less of something. Encourage your children to use water wisely, turn off lights when leaving a room, and use your own bags at the grocery store.

REUSE: Means to use an item again. Refill water bottles, wash dishes and containers instead of using disposable, mend or repair the things you have before buying new, and donate clothes and toys to be used by someone else.

RECYCLE: Means to make a new thing out of an old one. Recycle cans, bottles, and newspapers. Participate in local environmental initiatives like recycling drives.

REBUY: Means to purchase items that have already been used or recycled. Shop at thrift and consignment stores and when possible buy items that have been made from recycled materials.

IX

Summer Fitness Program

Choose a strength or cardio exercise for each day of academic activities. Check the box ✅ each day you complete your fitness activity. Fill in the Fitness Log on the back of each Incentive Contract Calendar. Choose exercises from the Health and Nutrition section in the back of the book. Exercise videos can be viewed at **www.SummerFitActivities.com.**

	Date	Stretch	Activity	Time
1.	*examples:* June 4	Run in place	Sky Reach	7 min
2.	June 5	Toe Touches	Bottle Curls	15 min
3.				
4.				
5.				

Let's Move!

Warm Up! Get ready to exercise by stretching and moving around.

Stretch! Move your head slowly side to side, try to touch each shoulder. Now move your head forward, touch your chin to your chest, then look up and as far back as you can. Try to touch your back with the back of your head.

Touch your toes when standing. Bend over at the waist and touch the end of your toes or the floor. Hold this position for 10 seconds.

Move! Walk or jog in place for 3-5 minutes to warm up before you exercise. Shake your arms and roll your shoulders when you are finished.

15. Circle the adjectives.

The small, gray mouse skittered across the tile floor and into its tiny hole.

16. Fill in the correct punctuation in each sentence.

a. Ouch that hurt

b. What time does the movie start

c. I am so happy to be on summer vacation

17. Write a synonym for each word. Ex. Glad= happy

a. scared = _____   b. wise = _____   c. finish = _____

18. Write an antonym for each word. Ex. In= out

a. above = _____   b. dark = _____   c. cold = _____

19 Circle the letters that should be capitalized in this sentence.

My aunt megan lives in seattle, washington.

20. Add commas where needed.

John Joseph and Gabe went camping in the mountains.

21. Write these words in alphabetical order.

freedom   factory   giant   harbor   group

_____, _____, _____, _____, _____

22. Circle the correct homophone.

a. Sam got a new (pair, pear) of shoes for his birthday.

b. I (read, red) the book I got from the library all afternoon.

23. Write the contraction for each set of words.

a. I will = _____ b. you are = _____ c. it is = _____

24. Make each singular word plural.

a. wolf = _____ b. baby = _____ c. girl = _____

25. Add the correct suffix –ful, -est, -ing, -er.

a. Paulo is tall _____ than his brother Chad.

b. Sam is the tall_____ boy on the basketball team.

c. I like sing_____ in the shower.

Read the paragraph and answer the questions.

Neil Armstrong was an astronaut. In 1969, he did something nobody had done before when he walke on the moon. When he first stepped on the moon, he said, "One small step for man, one giant leap fc mankind."

26. Circle the main idea of this paragraph.

a. The Phases of the moon   b. Rockets.   c. Who first walked on the moon.

27. Circle the correct way to break astronaut into syllables.

as-tr-o-naut   a-str-o-naut   as-tro-naut   astr-o-naut

28. Write four words that rhyme with moon.

_____, _____, _____, _____.

29. Circle the correct choice.

a. I (am , are) going to the beach today.

b. What (does, do) the word complicate mean?

c. I saw (a, an) elephant at the zoo.

d. Please water the plants over (their, there).

(4)

INCENTIVE CONTRACT CALENDAR

My parents and I agree that if I complete this section of

Summer Fit Activities™

and read _____ minutes a day, my reward will be _____

Child Signature: _____   Parent Signature: _____

Day 1			Day 6		
Day 2			Day 7		
Day 3			Day 8		
Day 4			Day 9		
Day 5			Day 10		

 Color the for each day of activities completed.

 Color the for each day of reading completed.

Summer Fitness Log

Choose your exercise activity each day from the Aerobic and Strength Activities in the back of the book. Record the date, stretch, activity and how long you performed your exercise activity below. Fill in how many days you complete your fitness activity on your Incentive Contract Calendars.

	Date	Stretch	Activity	Time
examples:	June 4	Run in place	Sky Reach	7 min
	June 5	Toe Touches	Bottle Curls	15 min
1.				
2.				
3.				
4.				
5.				
6.				
7.				
8.				
9.				
10.				

I promise to do my best for me. I exercise to be healthy and active. I am awesome because I am me.

Child Signature: _____

Idioms

Idioms are words, phrases, or expressions that cannot be taken literally. They have a second meaning. For example, "Once in a blue moon" means not very often.

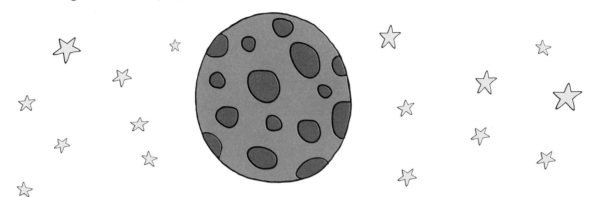

Read each sentence and circle the correct meaning of the idiom shown in quotations.

1.	Mom lets me stay up past midnight "once in a blue moon."
	all the time **Ex:** (not very often)
2.	After losing the tennis match, Mariah was "down in the dumps."
	in the garbage feeling bad
3.	My Grandpa "gets a kick out of" playing video games with me.
	enjoys it got kicked out
4.	Gabe told me I had won the contest but he was just "pulling my leg."
	grabbing my foot teasing me
5.	Dad couldn't "make heads or tails" out of the directions for the camera.
	see the picture understand
6.	Maddie was "playing with fire" when she was pulling the dog's tail.
	taking a risk playing with matches

Draw a line to match the idiom with the meaning.

7. Raining cats and dogs	Go to bed
8. Ants in your pants	Go ahead and eat
9. Hit the hay	Pouring rain
10. Your head is in the clouds	Easy
11. Chow down	Don't know what to say
12. Cat's got your tongue	Wiggling around
13. Piece of cake	Day dreaming

Rounding a number means you "bump" it up or down to a nearby number. The rules of rounding are simple.

If the number you are rounding is followed by a 5,6,7,8,or 9, round the number up. Ex: 38 = 40	If the number you are rounding is followed by a 0,1,2,3,or 4, round the number down. Ex: 34 = 30

Round to the nearest ten		Round to the nearest hundred	
58 = 60		345 = 300	
145 = 150		887 = 900	

1. 63 = _____

2. 168 = _____

3. 292 = _____

4. 359 = _____

5. 98 = _____

6. 387 = _____

7. 127 = _____

8. 765 = _____

9. 126 = _____

10. 156 = _____

11. 623 = _____

12. 3,975 = _____

13. 5,230 = _____

14. 8,432 = _____

Round to the nearest thousand.

15. 2,345 = _____

16. 7,620 = _____

17. 4,922 = _____

18. 1,120 = _____

19. 1,987 = _____

20. 5,450 = _____

21. 6,834 = _____

22. 9,876 = _____

23. 8,320 = _____

Choose your STRENGTH exercise!

Exercise for today:

_____

Day 1

Check & Record in Fitness Log.

- **Arachnophobia is the fear of spiders and is one of the most common fears of humans.**
- **Are you afraid of spiders? Learning about something can help you overcome your fears.**
- **Spiders have 48 knees.**
- **Tarantulas can live up to 30 years!**

Read the passage on spiders and answer the questions below.

A spider is an arachnid. Arachnids have four pairs of jointed legs and two distinct body parts, the head and abdomen. There are more than 30,000 species of spiders. Spiders come in all shapes, sizes, and colors, and while they may seem scary, most spiders are not harmful to humans. All spiders have eight legs, and as many as eight eyes. Spiders don't have ears but "hear" by feeling sound vibrations with the tiny hairs that cover their legs.

As spiders grow, they molt and leave their old tight skin behind when they grow a new one. Spiders can molt many times during their lifetime. Spiders live in hot and cold climates and live on every continent except Antarctica. Spiders can be found in many different places: houses, gardens, underground, and even in water. Not all spiders spin webs, but the ones that do spin silk thread from their spinnerets. Some spiders are poisonous, such as the black widow and the brown recluse, but most are harmless and spend their days eating insects, which would otherwise take over the planet!

1. A spider is an _____.

2. Describe the characteristic of a spider. _____.

3. How do spiders "hear"? _____

4. What is it called when spiders shed their own skin? _____

5. A spider spins a web with its _____.

6. A spider's two main body parts are the _____ and the _____.

Prime Numbers

A prime number is a whole number greater than 1 that has exactly two factors, 1 and itself. A composite number is a whole number that is greater than 1 and has more than two factors. The number 1 is a special case and is neither prime nor composite.

Circle all the prime numbers between 1 and 50. Hint: there are 15. Put a square around the number that is neither prime nor composite.

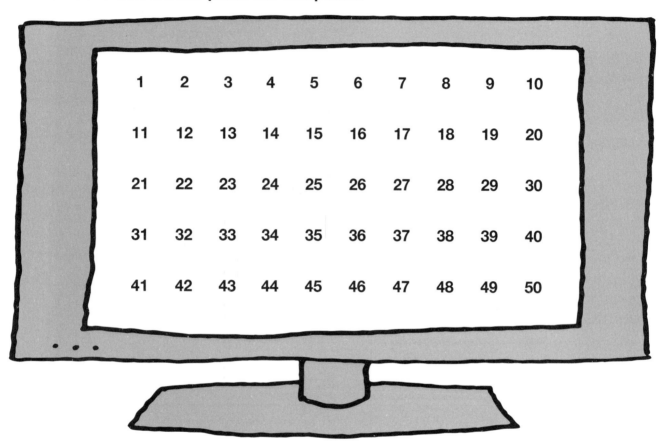

List 5 composite numbers between 1 and 50.

_____, _____, _____, _____, _____,

Day 2

Synonyms and Antonyms

Synonyms are words that have the same meaning as another word. Antonyms are words that have the opposite meaning.

Draw a line to match each word with its antonym.

Ex:

1. wet	loud
2. awake	go
3. happy	float
4. stop	dry
5. sink	white
6. black	sad
7. quiet	asleep

Write a synonym to replace each underlined word.

8. I sat on the <u>sofa</u> and read my book._____

9. Mom found a <u>giant</u> spider in the garden. _____

10. Albert Einstein was very <u>intelligent</u>. _____

11. I rode the roller coaster at the <u>carnival</u>. _____

12. Mr. Brown was <u>glad</u> when he found his lost dog, Spot._____

13. When I saw George up ahead, I <u>shouted</u> to get his attention. _____

Right Angle.	Obtuse Angle	Acute Angle
A right angle is a 90 degree angle and makes an L shape.	An obtuse angle is greater than 90 degrees.	An acute angle is a "cute little" angle that is less than 90 degrees.

Label each angle. Use 1 for right angles, 2 for obtuse angels and 3 for acute angles.

1. _____

2. _____

3. _____

4. _____

5. _____

6. _____

7. _____

8. _____

9. _____

Circle all the angles in the picture.

10. How many right angles?_____

11. How many obtuse angles? _____

12. How many acute angles?_____

Choose your STRENGTH exercise!

Day 3

Exercise for today:

_____

Check & Record in Fitness Log.

 **Amazing Adjectives**

 **Day 4**

Adjectives are descriptive words. Adjectives are used to describe or modify another person or thing in the sentence. Choose adjectives from the list to answer the questions.

ADJECTIVES				
honest	slimy	trustworthy	smelly	fast
pretty	creative	loving	beautiful	busy
lazy	hot	funny	clever	fuzzy
strong	kind	noisy	windy	colorful
sweet	juicy	rotten	studious	delicious

1. Choose 3 adjectives to describe your mother.

_____, _____, _____

2. What 2 adjectives describe a bag of garbage?

_____, _____

3. Choose 3 adjectives to describe what kind of student you are.

_____, _____, _____

4. Describe a summer day.

_____, _____, _____

5. What adjectives describe your best friend?

_____, _____, _____

6. Describe strawberries.

_____, _____, _____

Circle the adjectives in the following sentences.

7. Mom made a delicious dinner and chocolate cake for my 8th birthday.

8. The soft, furry hamster burrowed into his tiny nest.

9. I am wearing a striped shirt and my new, blue jeans to the circus.

Times Tables

Use the grid to fill in your time tables.

X	1	4	6	3	5	9	8	7	2	10
1. 3	3									
2. 6										
3. 9										
4. 4			12							
5. 1										
6. 5										
7. 7										
8. 2										
9. 10										
10. 8					72					

Use your completed times table to solve these problems.

11. $(10 \times 10) + (6 \times 5) + (2 \times 4) =$ _____

12. $(7 \times 7) + (3 \times 1) - (5 \times 2) =$ _____

Choose your AEROBIC exercise!

Day 4

Exercise for today:

_____

Check & Record in Fitness Log.

3–4 • © Summer Fit Activities™

HONESTY

Honesty means being fair, truthful, and trustworthy. Honesty means telling the truth no matter what. People who are honest do not lie, cheat, or steal.

Honest Abe

Abraham Lincoln was an honest man. He worked hard all his life and believed that being honest was very important. Lincoln was born in a log cabin on February 12, 1809. When he was only 9 years old, his mother died. Lincoln had to work hard to help his father so he wasn't able to go to school much. Instead he read books. Lincoln loved to read and learned a lot.

Lincoln became the 16th president of the United States of America. During his presidency he helped end slavery and kept the states together.

Use the words to fill in the blanks.

slavery	log	cabin	read	honesty	president

1. Abraham Lincoln was born in a _____.

2. He loved to _____ books.

3. Abraham was known for his _____.

4. Abraham Lincoln was the 16th _____ of the United States of America.

5. When he was president he helped end _____.

Value:

HONESTY

Being honest means to be truthful in what you say and do. It means that you do not lie, cheat or steal. Sometimes this can be difficult, especially when we are scared or ashamed about something we did. Sometimes it takes courage to be honest, especially when it is uncomfortable.

"Whatever you are, be a good one"
-Abe Lincoln

What does honesty look like? Choose an honest action below and draw a picture to represent it in the picture frame.

- I cheat on a test.
- I keep a promise.
- I play fair.
- I take a candy bar from the store without paying.
- I take money out of my dad's wallet without asking.
- I find $5.00 at the library and take it to the front desk.

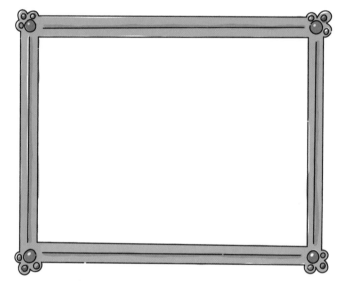

HONESTY PLEDGE

I promise to tell the truth every day. I will be honest in what I do and what I say.

_____

My Signature

How does it feel when someone lies to you?

_____

_____

_____

_____

Day 5

Choose a Play or Exercise Activity!

3–4 • © Summer Fit Activities™

Summer Explorer
Discover New Things to Play and Do!

- Visit the library and get a card if you do not have one.

- Make a fort out of blankets and sheets.

- Make a biodegradable bird feeder and hang it in the yard.

- Have a lemonade stand get your friends to help.

- Play flashlight tag.

- Visit a fire station. Does your family have a plan of what to do in case of fire? Plan a family fire drill.

- Sign up for a free summer reading program at your local bookstore.

- Go for a walk.

- Look up and find figures in the clouds.

- Play an outdoor game like "Simon Says" or "Kick the Can" with family or friends.

- Go for a bike ride.

- Pick up trash around your neighborhood and recycle.

- Find an ant colony. Drop some crumbs and observe what happens. Stay away from fire ants.

- Build a castle or fort out of Legos or blocks.

- Use a recycled plastic bag to create a parachute that will slowly fall to the ground.

- Watch a sunrise or sunset, paint a picture of it.

- Run through the sprinklers.

- Make S'mores and tell ghost stories under the stars.

- Create an obstacle course. Invite your friends and time them to see how fast they complete it.

Biodegradable Birdfeeder

 Collect your supplies: peanut butter, birdseed, oranges, and string for hanging.

 Tie a long string around the pinecone or toilet roll before spreading peanut butter on them and rolling in birdseed. Cut an orange in half, scoop out fruit and fill with birdseed. Attach strings to hang feeder in branch.

 Hang your bird treat in the yard and watch for your feathered friends to come and feast.

Summer Journal I

Write about your favorite outdoor summer activity.

Example: Camping, swimming or biking

3-4 • © Summer Fit Activities™

Plurals

A plural form of a word is needed when a word is used to describe more than one. Rewrite each word in its plural form.

Ex: peach	peaches
1. goose	
2. mouse	
3. box	
4. boy	
5. dog	
6. baby	
7. man	
8. puppy	
9. table	
10. calf	

11. coat	
12. fish	
13. watch	
14. wolf	
15. leaf	
16. lady	
17. bunny	
18. monkey	
19. dish	
20. letter	

Figures that are the same size and shape are congruent. Write yes or no if the shapes are congruent.

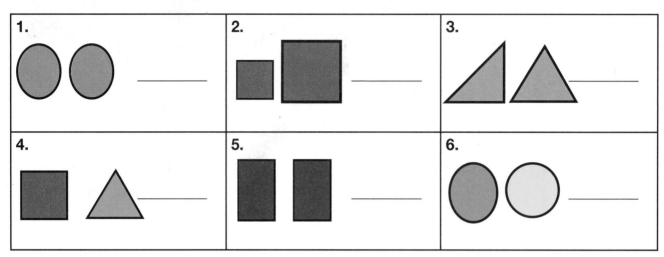

1.	2.	3.
4.	5.	6.

Circle the shapes that are congruent in each row.

7.

8.

9.

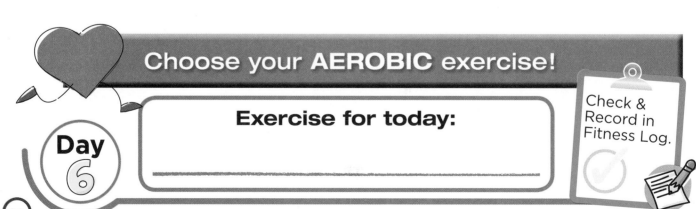

Choose your **AEROBIC** exercise!

Exercise for today:

Check & Record in Fitness Log.

Day 6

20

| am | is | will | are | were | was |

Fill in the blank with a helping verb from the box.

1. My friends and I _____are_____ have a picnic in the park tomorrow.

2. Today I _____Was_____ going swimming with my Aunt Megan.

3. We _____Were_____ fishing at the lake yesterday when it began to rain.

4. Tomorrow we _____am_____ going to the carnival.

5. The baby _____is_____ sleeping now so we must play quietly.

6. I _____will_____ riding my bike when I hit a rock and fell.

Possessive Pronouns

Some pronouns are used to show possession or ownership. Choose the possessive pronouns that best complete the sentence and write them on the line.

7. _____ mom planted flowers in the yard. (My/Mine) Gardening is _____ favorite hobby. (her/hers)

8. Grace finished _____ art project (her/hers) but Maddie will finish _____ tomorrow. (her/hers)

9. _____ family enjoys fishing and camping together. (Our/Ours)

10. Please remember to clean _____ room before you go outside to play. (your, yours)

11. Mr. and Mrs. Star painted _____ house. (their, theirs)

12. _____ sister was in a play last night. (My/Mine) It was _____ first time in a leading role. (her/hers)

13. Dad trimmed the apple tree in _____ yard (our/ours) because _____ branches were overgrown. (its/your)

14. My brother fell off _____ bike (his/hers) and broke _____ arm (his/hers).

15. Sally likes to wear _____ hair down (her/hers) but Judith likes to wear _____ in pony tails. (her/hers)

16. This cookie is _____ (my/mine) and that cookie is _____ (your/yours).

Roman numerals come from the numeral system of ancient Rome. It is based on some of the letters of the alphabet that can be combined to represent numbers that are the sum of their values.

I = 1	V = 5	X = 10	L=50	C=100

Draw a line from the Arabic numeral to the correct Roman numeral.

1. 6	VIII		5. 10	XIII
2. 8	II		6. 5	IX
3. 2	IV		7. 13	X
4. 4	VI		8. 9	V

9. Write the Arabic numeral for each Roman numeral.

XX _____	XVII _____	XIX _____
XXVII _____	C _____	IV _____
LXII _____	XL _____	XXIII _____

10. Write the Roman numeral for each Arabic numeral.

36 _____	55 _____	14 _____
29 _____	40 _____	21 _____

11. Fill in the missing Roman numerals.

I _____, III, _____, _____, VI, _____, _____, _____, X, _____, _____.

Choose your STRENGTH exercise!

Exercise for today:

_____

Check & Record in Fitness Log.

Day 7

The prefix re usually means do again. Rewrap means wrap again.	The prefix de usually means from, down, or away. Depart means go away from.
The prefix pre usually means before. Preview means view before.	The prefix ex usually means out of or from. Export means send out of.

Read each word, circle the prefix and write the root word on the line. Then write what the word means.

1. (re)wash **Ex.** _____ wash _____   _____ wash again _____

2. exchange _____   _____

3. rebuild _____   _____

4. decrease _____   _____

5. reteach _____   _____

6. detour _____   _____

7. preschool _____   _____

8. redo _____   _____

9. prepay _____   _____

10. exclaim _____   _____

Choose three words from the list above and put them into sentences.

11. _____

_____

12. _____

_____

13. _____

_____

Write the following in standard form.

1. Nine hundred twenty-five = _____

2. Seven thousand four hundred sixteen = _____

3. Three hundred seventy-five = _____

4. Two hundred fourteen = _____

Write in words.

5. 320 = _____

6. 1,852 = _____

7. 5,248 = _____

8. 3,980 = _____

Write in expanded form.

9. **Ex. 598 = 500 + 90 + 8**

10. 4,367 = _____

11. 6,781 = _____

12. 8,103 = _____

Write the number.

13. 1,000 + 700 + 40 +3 = _____

14. 3,000 + 500 + 20 +9 = _____

15. 9,000 + 200 + 60 +5 = _____

16. 5,000 + 900 + 80 +2 = _____

Write the number that is halfway between.

17. **Ex. 200, 400 = 300**

18. 500, 700= _____

19. 60, 70 = _____

20. 6,000, 8,000 = _____

21. 75, 95 = _____

22. 150, 250 = _____

Choose your AEROBIC exercise!

Exercise for today:

Check & Record in Fitness Log.

Day 8

Animal Riddles

Match each description with the correct animal in the sentences below.

capybara	**woodpecker**
hummingbird	**chameleon**
penguin	**raccoon**

1. My wings beat at 80-100 strokes per second. I get all my energy from the sugar in the nectar I drink. I am a _____.

2. I live among the trees and hammer into their trunks with my sharp bill to find insect larvae, sap, or to build a nest hole. I am a _____.

3. I am slow moving and rely on my ability to change color to protect myself. I live in a tree and use my flexible tail to cling to branches while I trap insects with my long, sticky tongue. I am a _____.

4. Even though I am a bird I cannot fly. My feet are powerful flippers and help me swim fast in the cold Antarctic Ocean. I am a _____.

5. I am the world's largest rodent and am the size of a sheep. I look like my relative the guinea pig and live in South America. I am a _____.

6. I live in North America and am easily recognized by my striped tail and black circles around my eyes. I like to raid garbage cans to look for food and am usually nocturnal. I am a_____
_____.

Stretch your brain.....
Name the two continents mentioned in the sentences above.

_____ , _____

Divide these words into syllables.

hummingbird   _____   _____   _____

woodpecker   _____   _____   _____

capybara   _____   _____   _____   _____

Parts of a whole.

 How many parts are shaded?   2   How many parts in all?   3

The shaded part is   2/3   The unshaded part is   1/3

Write the fraction that shows the shaded part in the different shapes.

1.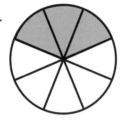

2.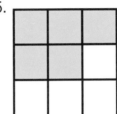

3.

Ex: 3/8   _____   _____

4.

5.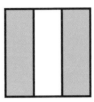

6.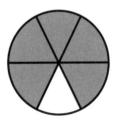

_____   _____   _____

Write <, >, or = for the fractions below.

7. 1/2 circle _____ 2/4 circle   8. 1/4 square _____ 3/4 square

Shade the fraction of each shape.

9.   **3/5**   10.   **2/3**   11.   **7/10**

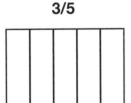   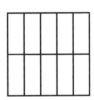

 Choose your **STRENGTH** exercise!

Exercise for today:

_____

Day 9

 Check & Record in Fitness Log.

Compassion is caring about the feelings and needs of others.

Mother Teresa

As a young woman Mother Teresa decided she wanted to be a missionary in order to spread love and compassion in the world. Mother Teresa spent her life taking care of people in India who had nobody to take care of them including the poor, orphaned and sick. She took care of thousands of people who were unwanted and unloved and she did it without asking for anything in return. Mother Teresa showed compassion because she always put the interest of others in front of her own. Even when she was suffering from illness, she continued to care for others and never gave up on her goal of helping all those in need.

Write three examples of how someone has shown compassion to you.

1. _____

2. _____

3. _____

Write three examples of how you have shown compassion to others.

4. _____

5. _____

6. _____

Value:

COMPASSION

Having compassion means showing kindness, caring and a willingness to help others who may be sick, hurt, poor, or in need. When you have compassion you are putting yourself in someone else's shoes and really feeling for them. You can do this in very small ways for example when your friend trips and falls. You can do this in larger ways when someone you know does not have enough food to eat.

"Love and compassion are necessities not luxuries. Without them, humanity cannot survive."

– Dalai Lama

Unscramble the letters to reveal the traits of being a Hero of Compassion.

dnik

ufltuhgtoh

aricgn

udantnesinrgd

epilngh

ielgnsnti

rstceandoei

ronfmoicgt

avber

tpaenti

Make a "Compassion Jar". Cut out several slips of paper and write on each a way to show compassion. For example: Hold the door for someone, smile at a stranger, or read to a younger child. Choose one to do each day.

(patient) (brave) (comforting) (considerate) (listening)
(helping) (understanding) (caring) (thoughtful) (kind)

Day 10

Choose a Play or Exercise Activity!

INCENTIVE CONTRACT CALENDAR

My parents and I agree that if I complete this section of

Summer Fit Activities™

and read _____ minutes a day, my reward will be _____

Child Signature: _____   Parent Signature: _____

Day 1			Day 6		
Day 2			Day 7		
Day 3			Day 8		
Day 4			Day 9		
Day 5			Day 10		

Color the for each day of activities completed.

Color the for each day of reading completed.

Summer Fitness Log

Choose your exercise activity each day from the Aerobic and Strength Activities in the back of the book. Record the date, stretch, activity and how long you performed your exercise activity below. Fill in how many days you complete your fitness activity on your Incentive Contract Calendars.

	Date	Stretch	Activity	Time
examples:	June 4	Run in place	Sky Reach	7 min
	June 5	Toe Touches	Bottle Curls	15 min
1.				
2.				
3.				
4.				
5.				
6.				
7.				
8.				
9.				
10.				

I promise to do my best for me. I exercise to be healthy and active. I am awesome because I am me.

Child Signature: _____

Poetry Corner

Read the poem aloud and answer the questions below.

Where Go The Boats?
By Robert Louis Stevenson

Dark brown I the river,
Golden is the sand,
It flows along forever,
With trees on either hand.

Green leaves afloating,
Castles of the foam,
Boats of mine a - boating -
Where will all come home?

On goes the river,
And out past the mill,
Away down the valley,
Away down the hill.

Away down the river,
A hundred miles or more,
Other little children
Shall bring my boats ashore.

Robert Louis Stevenson

Extra Credit: Look up the poet Robert Louis Stevenson. Find out when he lived and where he was from. Read some of his other poems such as "Foreign Lands", "Bed in Summer", and - "My Bed is a Boat" Try to memorize the poem "Where go the Boats".

1. What do you think this poem is about? _____

2. What are the adjectives used to describe the river in the first stanza? _____

3. What are the plural words in the second stanza?

_____, _____, _____.

4. After reading the third stanza, are the boats in the poem going far away or not too far?

_____ .

5. What are the rhyming words in the last stanza? _____, _____.

6. Do you like this poem? _____ Why or why not? _____

_____

Monster Multiplication Review. Multiply to find your answers.

1. 3 x 4 _____   3 x 5 _____   3 x 10 _____   3 x 9 _____   3 x 2 _____

3 x 6 _____   3 x 8 _____   3 x 1 _____   3 x 7 _____   3 x 3 _____

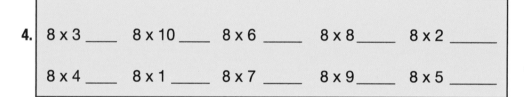

2. 6 x 6 _____   6 x 2 _____   6 x 5 _____   6 x 4 _____   6 x 9 _____

6 x 3 _____   6 x 7 _____   6 x 10 _____   6 x 8 _____   6 x 1 _____

3. 4 x 5 _____   4 x 3 _____   4 x 1 _____   4 x 10 _____   4 x 6 _____

4 x 2 _____   4 x 7 _____   4 x 4 _____   4 x 9 _____   4 x 8 _____

4. 8 x 3 _____   8 x 10 _____   8 x 6 _____   8 x 8 _____   8 x 2 _____

8 x 4 _____   8 x 1 _____   8 x 7 _____   8 x 9 _____   8 x 5 _____

5. 5 x 10 _____   5 x 1 _____   5 x 6 _____   5 x 2 _____   5 x 4 _____

5 x 8 _____   5 x 7 _____   5 x 3 _____   5 x 9 _____   5 x 5 _____

6. 7 x 3 _____   7 x 2 _____   7 x 8 _____   7 x 9 _____   7 x 5 _____

7 x 7 _____   7 x 4 _____   7 x 6 _____   7 x 1 _____   7 x 10 _____

Choose your STRENGTH exercise!

Check & Record in Fitness Log.

Exercise for today:

_____

Day 1

 **Nouns**

 **Day 2**

A noun is a name of a person, place, or thing.
Write **PERSON, PLACE,** or **THING** beside each noun.

1. car _____

2. chair _____

3. bank _____

4. nurse _____

5. mouse _____

6. library _____

7. fireman _____

8. baby _____

9. kitchen _____

10. book _____

11. park _____

12. teacher _____

13. brother _____

14. moon _____

15. restaurant _____

A proper noun is a specific person, place, or thing. Proper nouns always begin with a capital letter.

Write a common noun for each proper noun.

16. Toy Story = movie

17. September _____

18. Arizona _____

19. Christmas _____

20. Bob's Pet Store _____

21. Maple Avenue _____

22. Poodle _____

23. James _____

Write a proper noun for each common noun.

24. weekday _____

25. state _____

26. store _____

27. teacher _____

28. girl _____

29. month _____

30. country _____

31. school _____

Mixed practice. Add and subtract to find your answers.

| **1.** | 289 − 146 | **3.** | 334 + 215 | **5.** | 678 - 427 | **7.** | 521 - 310 |

| **2.** | 430 + 268 | **4.** | 765 - 231 | **6.** | 978 − 426 | **8.** | 152 + 137 |

Fill in the missing number to complete the equation.

Ex: 6 x __5__ = 30	**9.** _____ x 9 = 18	**10.** 5 x 8 =_____	**11.** 3 x _____= 21
12. 6 x 8 = _____	**13.** 7 x _____ = 35	**14.** 2 x _____ = 20	**15.** _____ x 6= 24
16. 4 x 9 = _____	**17.** 9 x _____ = 27	**18.** _____ x 5 = 20	**19.** 4 x 4 = _____

Finish the counting patterns.

20. 50, 45, _____, _____, _____, _____, _____, _____, _____, _____, 0

21. 20, 22, 24, _____, _____, _____, _____, _____, _____, _____, _____

22. 12, 15, _____, _____, _____, _____, _____, _____, _____, _____

23. 130, 140, _____, _____, _____, _____, _____, _____, _____, _____

Choose your AEROBIC exercise!

Exercise for today:

_____

Day 2

Check & Record in Fitness Log.

Nouns and Verbs

Nouns are words that name a person, place, or thing. Verbs are action words. Circle the verbs and underline the nouns.

1.

run	cloud	swim	dog	eat	jump
fence	boy	hop	sing	apple	drink
whisper	house	spider	crawl	tree	bark

Verbs can tell what is happening now (present), what happened yesterday (past), and what will happen tomorrow (future). Use the correct verb to complete each sentence.

2. Swim, swam, will swim. We like to _____.

We _____ yesterday.

We _____ at the lake next week.

3. Play, played, will play   I _____ baseball every day with my friends.

I _____ baseball with my dad last Saturday.

I _____ baseball with my uncle tomorrow.

4. Sing, sang, will sing   I like to _____ in the shower.

I _____ to the baby last night.

I _____ in the choir on Sunday.

5. Draw, drew, will draw   The artist likes to _____ kids at the zoo.

Sam _____ a picture for the art show next week.

I _____ a picture for my grandma tomorrow

Adding Multiple Numbers

1.	64	2.	52	3.	76	4.	39
	34		30		24		16
	+ 22		+ 15		+ 48		+ 25

Add.

5. 5 + 6 + 4 + 9 = _____	7. 5 + 1 + 4 + 2 = _____	9. 8 + 5 + 2 + 7 = _____
6. 9 + 3 + 1 + 7 = _____	8. 6 + 4 + 7 + 3 = _____	10. 8 + 5 + 2 + 4 = _____

Write the numbers that come before, between, or after.

11. 49, _____, 51	14. _____, 19, 20	17. _____, 5,000, _____
12. 99, _____, 101	15. 348, _____, 350	18. 8,999, _____
13. _____, 300, _____	16. 1, 276, _____	19. 999, _____, 1,001

What time is it?

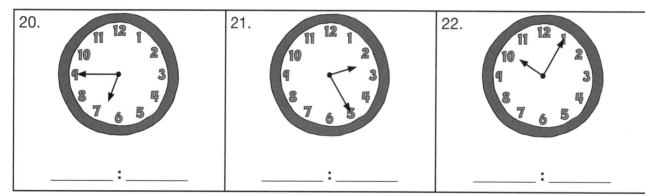

20.	21.	22.
_____ : _____	_____ : _____	_____ : _____

Choose your STRENGTH exercise!

Check & Record in Fitness Log.

Day 3

Exercise for today:

_____

3–4 • © Summer Fit Activities™

Homophones

Homophones are words that sound the same but have different meanings and spellings. Choose the correct homophone for each sentence. Circle it and write it on the line.

1. The dog wagged its _____ when I gave him a bone.   (tale, tail)

2. My brother's birthday is next _____.   (week, weak)

3. I ate _____ much candy, and now I feel sick.   (to, two, too)

4. I _____ two library books yesterday.   (read, red)

5. Do you _____ your times tables?   (no, know)

6. It is important to _____ thank you notes.   (right, write)

7. _____ do you go camping?   (Wear, Where)

8. The recipe calls for 2 cups of _____ and 1 cup of sugar.   (flower, flour)

9. My library books are _____ on Thursday.   (dew, due)

10. There was snow on the mountain _____.   (peak, peek)

11. A _____ chicken is called a rooster, while a female is a hen.   (mail, male)

12. There was a _____ under the sink, so my mom called the plumber.   (leek, leak)

3-4 • © Summer Fit Activities™

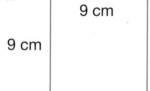

Perimeter

A perimeter is the total distance around a shape.   Write the perimeter of each shape.

1.

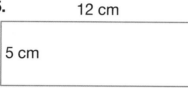
6 cm

2 cm

_____

2.

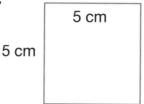
5 cm

5 cm

_____

3.

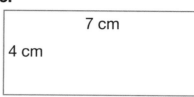
7 cm

4 cm

_____

4.

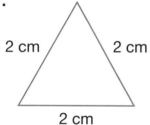
9 cm

9 cm

_____

5.

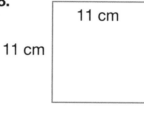
12 cm

5 cm

_____

6.

5 cm   5 cm

5 cm

_____

7.

2 cm   2 cm

2 cm

_____

8.

11 cm

11 cm

_____

9.

20 cm

6 cm

_____

10. Use a ruler to draw a square with a perimeter of 8 cm.

Choose your AEROBIC exercise!

Exercise for today:

Check & Record in Fitness Log.

Day 4

3-4 • © Summer Fit Activities™

38

SummerFitActivities.com

TRUSTWORTHINESS

Value

Trustworthiness is being worthy of trust. It means people can count on you. You are honest and you keep your word.

Harriet Tubman was a slave before the Civil War. Being a slave meant that she had no property, no rights, and had to do whatever her master told her. Harriet had to work hard but even as a little girl she dreamed of being free. Although she was small, Harriet was strong and even more strong-willed. When she was an adult, Harriet escaped to the North where she was free. Being free herself wasn't enough for Harriet. She wanted other slaves to be free as well. Harriet led hundreds of slaves to freedom using the "Underground Railroad" which was a secret system of hiding places to help slaves escape. At one time there was a $40,000 reward offered by slave owners for her capture. Each time she went back to help more slaves, she risked her life. People trusted Harriet with their lives and she never let them down.

Being trustworthy is difficult because it includes having to display several characteristics including; HONESTY, COURAGE, FRIENDSHIP AND being RELIABLE.

Below, write a short sentence next to each word telling how Harriet Tubman displayed each of these characteristics.

1. Honesty (does not lie cheat or steal): _____

2. Courage (do what is right even when it is difficult):

_____

3. Friendship (do not betray someone's trust):

_____

4. Reliable (keep promises and follow through on commitment):

_____

5. Which of these qualities is your strongest? _____

6. Which of these qualities is your weakest? _____

Value: TRUSTWORTHINESS

FAMILY ACTIVITIES

Let's talk about it...

Talk with your child about keeping a promise. Help them to understand that it is important to think before they promise something. Be consistent when you are making promises to your children either in rewards or punishments. Lead by example and make sure to follow through with what you say.

Choose one or more activities to do with your family or friends.

 Talk about ways you show you are trustworthy. Remember that when you are dishonest and not truthful, people will not trust you. Think about the times you have been trustworthy. Write down at least 5 words that describe how you felt being trusted.

 Talk about what it means to be a trustworthy friend. Make a Friendship bracelet and give it to one of your friends. Let them know they can count on you to be a good friend.

 Write down the word TRUSTWORTHY. How many little words can you make from the letters?

VALUES ARE A FAMILY AFFAIR

Read more about
TRUSTWORTHINESS

Courage of Sarah Noble
By Alice Dalgliesh

Twenty and Ten
By Puffi n Book

After the Goat Man
By Betsy Byars

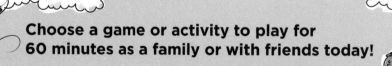

Choose a game or activity to play for 60 minutes as a family or with friends today!

Day 5

Choose a Play or Exercise Activity!

Summer Explorer

Discover New Things to Play and Do!

- Play in the rain. Make mud pies and jump in puddles.

- Have a book exchange with your friends.

- Finger paint.

- Make your own musical instruments out of cardboard boxes and perform a song.

- Create a healthy dinner menu for your family.

- Visit a lake, river, or pond. Bring a notebook to do some nature drawings.

- Make your own bubble solution. Go outside and make some enormous bubbles.

- Pick wildflowers and arrange them in a glass or jar.

- Draw a flipbook.

- Make cookies for a neighbor — deliver them with a parent.

- Go to the park with a friend.

- Sign up for a free project at Home Depot, Lowes, or Michaels.

- Make a scavenger hunt to do with friends or family.

- Plant something: flowers, vegetables, herbs, a tree.

- Read to a younger sibling.

- Make a photo album or scrapbook.

- Try a new cookie recipe.

- Have a water balloon fight.

- Help an elderly neighbor weed his/her garden.

- Paint or draw a self-portrait.

Giant Bubbles

6 cups Water
1/2 cup Dish Soap (Dawn blue)
1/2 cup Cornstarch
1 TBSP Baking Powder
1 TBSP Glycerin
(Glycerin found in cake decoration aisle at craft store)

1 Slowly mix together in large bucket or dishpan.

2 Let solution sit for 1-2 hours.

3 Tie a length of string between two straws to make a bubble wand or use store bought wands. The bigger your wand, the bigger your bubbles!

3-4 • © Summer Fit Activities™

Summer Journal II

Write about your family vacation.

 **Analogies**

An analogy is a comparison of similarities. Fill in the missing words to complete the analogies. : = "is to" and :: = "as".

Example: Puppy : dog :: cat : kitten = Puppy is to dog as cat is to kitten.

1. up : down :: in : _____

2. airplane : air :: ship : _____

3. boy : man :: girl : _____

4. wolf : pack :: fish : _____

5. smile : happy :: frown : _____

6. apple : fruit :: broccoli : _____

7. sun : day :: moon : _____

8. hand : arm :: foot : _____

9. eye : see :: ear : _____

10 fire : hot :: ice : _____

11. write : letter :: read : _____

12. calf : cow :: lamb : _____

Count the money and write the amount. Remember your dollar sign ($) and decimal point (.).

1.	
2.	
3.	
4.	

Answer the story problems by writing the amount.

5. I have 2 quarters and 3 nickels less than $1.00. _____

6. I have 3 quarters and 2 dimes more than $5.00. _____

7. Draw a picture to show $3.62.

Make dollars and cents then read each amount.

8.

Ex. 89 $ .89   125 _____   670 _____   1050 _____   1500 _____

5975 _____   2550 _____   09 _____   1246 _____   10065 _____

Choose your AEROBIC exercise!

Exercise for today:

Check & Record in Fitness Log.

Suffixes and Prefixes

Root Word	Prefix	Suffix
A root word is a word you can make into a new word by adding a beginning or an ending.	A prefix is a word part added to the beginning of a root word to create a word with a different meaning.	A suffix is a word part added to the end of a root word to create a word with a different meaning.

Prefix & Suffix: beginnings & endings

un = not	ful = full of	less = without
re = again	er = one who	dis = not

Read each root word and add the suffix. Write the new word on the line.

1. pay + ment = payment

2. wash + able = _____

3. fright + en = _____

4. break + able = _____

5. invent + ion = _____

6. improve + ment = _____

7. soft + en = _____

8. direct + ion = _____

Add a suffix to make a new word.

ness	ing	er	ed	est
ful		less		ly

9. collect _____

10. care _____

11. fear _____

12 loud _____

13. fast _____

14. walk _____

15. glad _____

16. neat _____

17. thought _____

18. cheat _____

19. sleep _____

20. safe _____

Write the root word on the line. Underline the prefix, circle the suffix

21. **Ex:** <u>un</u>happi⟨ness⟩   ____happy____

22. unpacking _____

23. defrosted _____

24. repainted _____

25. incorrectly _____

26. exclaimed _____

27. imperfectly _____

28. uncomfortable _____

Place Value

Look at the numbers and solve the riddle.

5,650	56	506	1,560

1. I have a 6 in the ten's place. _____

2. I am greater than 5,000. _____

3. I have a 6 in the hundred's place. _____

4. I have a zero in the ten's place. _____

5. I am less than 100. _____.

Write the value of the 6.

6. 1,652 = _____   7. 68 = _____   8. 6,349 = _____   9. 206 = _____

Write the value of the 5.

10. 52 = _____   11. 1,500 = _____   12. 895 = _____   13. 5,902 = _____

Write the value of the 2.

14. 129 = _____   15. 248 = _____   16. 72 = _____   17. 2,076 = _____

18. Put these numbers in order from smallest to largest.

652	568	89	129	1,067

Choose your STRENGTH exercise!

Check & Record in Fitness Log.

Exercise for today:

_____

Day 7

The Human Skeleton

Read the following passage on skeletons. Then answer the questions below.

The human skeleton has over 200 bones! Bones are the framework of your body. Your skeleton supports you and gives your body its shape. Your skeleton helps your body to move by giving your muscles a place to attach, these are called joints. Joints can be fixed, hinged, or ball and socket. The skeleton is also a shield. It protects soft organs such as the brain, heart, and lungs from injury.

The outside layer of bones is hard and made up of calcium and other minerals. Inside, bones are filled with a soft, fatty tissue called bone marrow. Your bone marrow has the very important job of making new blood cells for your body. The largest bone in the human body is the thigh bone, or femur. The smallest bone is called the stirrup bone, and is located inside your ear. When a bone is broken, new blood vessels grow. These eventually turn to bone. New marrow forms inside the bone and soon the bone is healed.

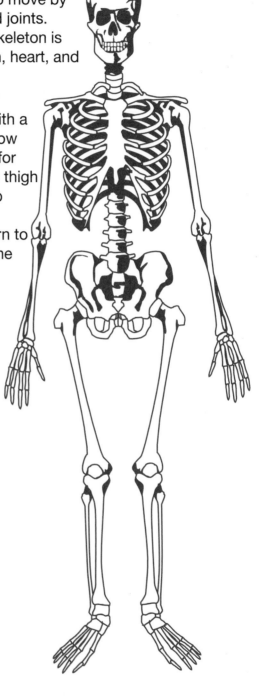

1. The body has more than _____

bones.

2. _____ makes up the hard outer

layer of bones.

3. Your skeleton protects soft organs like the

_____, _____,

and the _____.

4. The soft tissue inside your bones is called

_____.

5. Bone marrow makes new _____.

6. The largest bone is the _____.

7. Circle the plural words in the passage above.

How many did you find?_____

Write the digital time. Add 30 minutes. What time is it now?

1.

2.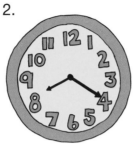

3.

4.

Ex: 7:46
_____

8:16
_____

_____

_____

_____

_____

_____

_____

5.

6.

7.

8.

_____

_____

_____

_____

_____

_____

_____

_____

Use words to write the time.

9.

Ex: 3:18 = eighteen minutes after three.

10.

2:55 = _____
_____
_____

11.

7:29 = _____
_____
_____

12.

9:35 = _____
_____
_____

Choose your **AEROBIC** exercise!

Exercise for today:

Check & Record in Fitness Log.

Day 8

_____

Antonyms

Antonyms are words with opposite meanings, like tall and short. Match words from the box to their antonym.

clean	near	low	in	down	hot	over
happy	careful	laugh	walk	whisper	hard	dark

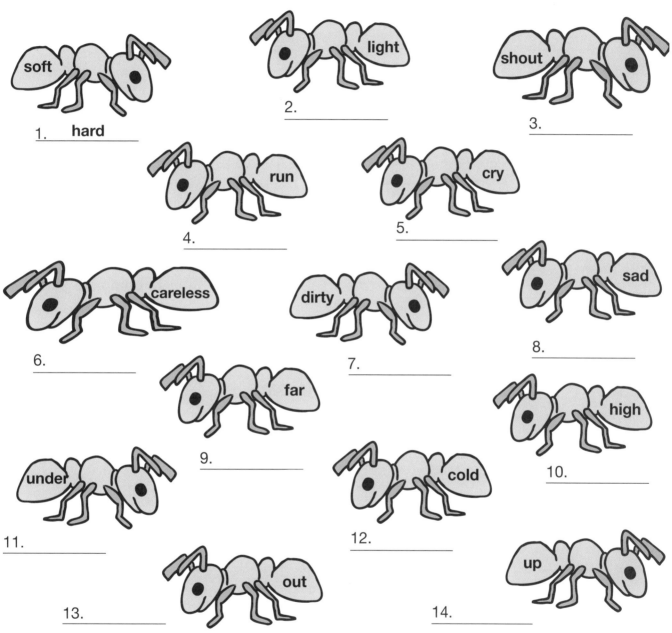

soft

1. hard

light

2. _____

shout

3. _____

run

4. _____

cry

5. _____

careless

6. _____

dirty

7. _____

sad

8. _____

far

9. _____

high

10. _____

under

11. _____

cold

12. _____

out

13. _____

up

14. _____

Think of an antonym for each underlined word.

15. A green light means <u>go</u> while a red light means _____.

16. I fell <u>asleep</u> before midnight on New Year's Eve, but my brothers stayed _____.

17. Everyone likes to <u>win</u>, but nobody likes to _____.

Race to the Finish

Fast Facts. Time yourself to see how fast you can complete these addition and subtraction problems.

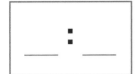

START TIME
Ready - Set - Go!

1. 5,634
+ 2,367
———

2. 4,328
+ 2,134
———

3. 9,902
+ 2,345
———

4. 1,200
+ 1,052
———

5. 5,648
– 3,246
———

6. 6,840
- 2,420
———

7. 9,864
– 6,342
———

8. 3,452
– 1,260
———

STOP TIME

**Total time
to complete**

Add 10 to each number.

9. 67 _____	11. 89 _____	13. 520 _____	15. 248 _____
10. 130 _____	12. 165 _____	14. 99 _____	16. 607 _____

Add 100 to each number.

17. 567 _____	19. 489 _____	21. 78 _____	23. 9,690 _____
18. 109 _____	20. 934 _____	22. 333 _____	24. 1,564 _____

Choose your STRENGTH exercise!

Exercise for today:

_____

Check &
Record in
Fitness Log.

Day 9

SummerFitActivities.com

3-4 • © Summer Fit Activities™

Self-discipline is to have control of your actions to improve and reach your goals. Self-discipline includes self-control, dedication and commitment.

Stephanie Lopez Cox works hard to reach her goals. Through self-discipline and dedication she played on the U.S. National Women's Soccer Team that won the gold medal at the 2008 Beijing Olympics. Stephanie practices very hard and is committed to doing what it takes to become the best athlete, soccer player and person she can be. Stephanie is known for her soccer skills, but also focused hard on her classes to earn a 3.76 grade point average in college. Stephanie knows what it takes to reach her goals and follows through even when it is not easy. She is disciplined as an athlete and at the same time is committed to helping others in need. Stephanie grew up in a home that fostered children; she uses the same focus and commitment that made her into a premier athlete, to help others by raising awareness for foster kids. Stephanie is dedicated to bettering the world around her through her childhood experiences and her current job as a professional athlete.

Answer true or false for each statement.

1. Stephanie doesn't work very hard. _____

2. She won a gold medal in the 2008 Olympics. _____

3. Stephanie was not a good student and got bad grades. _____

4. She tries to be a good person and a good athlete. _____

5. Stephanie helps foster children. _____

6. Stephanie only cares about herself and not others. _____

Value: SELF-DISCIPLINE

FAMILY ACTIVITIES

Choose one or more activities to do with your family or friends.

 Plan to exercise together as a family this week. Have a family walk after dinner. Choose an activity to do together. Hike, bike, swim, dance and play together. At night, play a game of "flashlight tag." Whoever gets "tagged" by the light is "it."

 Give up TV for a day, a week, or longer. Instead, spend time outside, reading, or with family and friends.

 Plan a sequence of events or activities to do in one day. Before you move on to the next one you must finish the one before it.

VALUES ARE A FAMILY AFFAIR

Read more about SELF-DISCIPLINE

The Book of Virtues
By William Bennet

Sign of the Beaver
By Elizabeth George Speare

From the Mixed Up Files of Mrs. Basil E. Frankweiler
By E. L. Konigsburg

Choose a game or activity to play for 60 minutes as a family or with friends today!

Day 10

Choose a **Play** or **Exercise** Activity!

INCENTIVE CONTRACT CALENDAR

My parents and I agree that if I complete this section of

Summer Fit Activities™

and read _____ minutes a day, my reward will be _____

Child Signature: _____   Parent Signature: _____

Day 1	✏️	📖	Day 6	✏️	📖
Day 2	✏️	📖	Day 7	✏️	📖
Day 3	✏️	📖	Day 8	✏️	📖
Day 4	✏️	📖	Day 9	✏️	📖
Day 5	✏️	📖	Day 10	✏️	📖

Color the for each day of activities completed.

Color the for each day of reading completed.

Summer Fitness Log

Choose your exercise activity each day from the Aerobic and Strength Activities in the back of the book. Record the date, stretch, activity and how long you performed your exercise activity below. Fill in how many days you complete your fitness activity on your Incentive Contract Calendars.

	Date	Stretch	Activity	Time
examples:	June 4	Run in place	Sky Reach	7 min
	June 5	Toe Touches	Bottle Curls	15 min
1.				
2.				
3.				
4.				
5.				
6.				
7.				
8.				
9.				
10.				

I promise to do my best for me. I exercise to be healthy and active. I am awesome because I am me.

Child Signature: _____

Sentence Structure

Rewrite the sentences using correct punctuation and capitalization.

1. joseph had a sleepover with his friends Brendan Jacob and sam

_____

_____

2. i am going to visit my friend isabella in san diego california

_____

_____

3. ouch a mosquito bit me on the leg

_____

_____

4. christmas is my favorite holiday said beth

_____

_____

5. mom packed us a delicious picnic lunch of sandwiches chips carrot sticks and cookies

_____

_____

6. grandmas favorite hobby is water skiing on bear lake

_____

_____

Combine the two sentences to make one sentence.

7. Jonathan went to the circus on Saturday. Noah went to the circus on Saturday.

_____

_____

8. Amy watered the plants in the garden. Amy pulled the weeds in the garden.

_____

_____

9. Ants use their antennae to smell and touch. Ants use their antennae to find food.

_____

_____

Draw an array then write a division sentence. Solve the equation.

25 triangles in 5 rows

Divide.

1. 48 ÷ 6 = _____

2. 30 ÷ 5 = _____

3. 16 ÷ 4 = _____

4. 27 ÷ 9 = _____

5. 42 ÷ 6 = _____

6. 81 ÷ 9 = _____

7. 24 ÷ 6 = _____

8. 40 ÷ 8= _____

9. 28 ÷ 7 = _____

Divide.

10. 6 | 32

11. 7 | 427

12. 8 | 78

13. 2 | 64

14. 4 | 95

15. 5 | 795

16. 3 | 654

17. 3 | 2,532

Choose your STRENGTH exercise!

Exercise for today:

Day 1

Use the map of the Western
United States of America to
answer the questions.

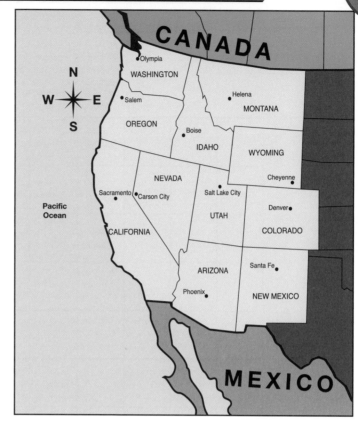

1. What state is East of Oregon?

_____

2. What is the capital of
Washington?

_____

3. Salt Lake City is the capital of
what state?

_____

4. Begin in Nevada, go east one
state and then directly south. What state are you in?

_____

5. What country is USA's neighbor to the North? _____

6. Which Western state is the biggest? _____

7. What ocean borders California? _____

8. What is the capital of Oregon? _____

9. What are the five states that share a border with Arizona? _____

_____

10. The capital of this state is Santa Fe? _____

Number Pairs

Connect the dots. What shape do you see?

Example: 2 across, 6 up

| 2, 7 |
| 3, 5 |
| 3, 8 |
| 4, 8 |
| 5, 7 |
| 6, 8 |
| 7, 8 |
| 8, 7 |
| 8, 6 |
| 7, 5 |
| 6, 4 |
| 5, 3 |
| 4, 4 |

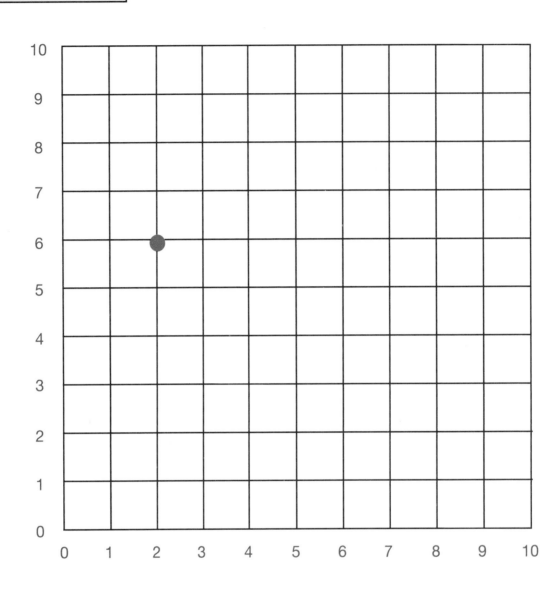

Connect the dots, what shape do you see? _____

Choose your AEROBIC exercise!

Exercise for today:

Check & Record in Fitness Log.

Day 2

3-4 • © Summer Fit Activities™

A syllable is a part of a word with a distinct vowel sound (a,e,i,o,u). The number of times you hear a vowel is the number of syllables you hear.

Look at each word. Write the number of vowels you see, the number of vowels you hear, and how many syllables the word has.

Word	Vowels Seen	Vowels Heard	Number of Syllables
1. **Ex:** monkey	2	2	2
2. hippopotamus			
3. wolf			
4. anteater			
5. alligator			
6. tiger			
7. elephant			
8. zebra			
9. rhinoceros			

Circle where would you look to find the number of syllables in a word?

dictionary	encyclopedia	atlas

In each row, circle the word that I divided into syllables correctly.

10. b-an-ana   ba-na-na   ban-an-a

11. be-cause   bec-ause   b-e-cause

12. fl-ow-ers   fl-ower-s   flow-ers

13. neigh-bor-ly   ne-igh-borl-y   neigh-bo-rly

14. wood-pecker   wood-peck-er   wood-pe-cker

Divide each word into syllables.

15. sweater _____

16. bookcase _____

17. realize _____

18. happiness _____

Add, subtract, multiply, or divide.

1. 234
    x 21
    _____

2. 3,029
    - 1,652
    _____

3. 2,432
    + 3,879
    _____

4. 809
    x 52
    _____

5. 6,723
    x 15
    _____

6. 9,422
    - 6,830
    _____

7. 2,652
    x 130
    _____

8. 2 ⟌ 1,470

Fill in the blanks to convert the measurements.

9. 1 ft. = _____ in.

12. 1 yd. = _____ ft.

15. 1 hr. = _____ min.

10. 1 da. = _____ hr.

13. 1 qt. = _____ pt.

16. 1 yd. = _____ in.

11. 1 week = _____ da.

14. 4 qt. = _____ gal.

17. 1 pt. = _____ c.

Choose your STRENGTH exercise!

Day 3

Exercise for today:

_____

Check & Record in Fitness Log.

The Water Cycle

Have you ever stood in the rain and let the raindrops fall onto your head and trickle down your face? Did you ever wonder where this water comes from? Every day the heat from the sun evaporates water from oceans, ponds, and lakes. When the sun heats up the earth, the warm air rises and begins to cool. This cooling of the air causes cloud to form and is called condensation. Condensation is the state of water when it changes from a gas to a liquid.

When these clouds reach colder air rain, snow, hail, or sleet fall to the earth and the process of evaporation begins again. This state of water when it falls to the earth is precipitation. The earth and air are constantly exchanging water with each other. This is called the water cycle.

Answer the questions below. Circle the correct answer, write it in the blank.

1. The source of energy that heats the earth is _____.

clouds	moon	rain	sun

2. Rain, snow, hail, and sleet are forms of _____.

condensation	precipitation	energy	wind

3. The state of water when it changes from a gas to a liquid is called_____.

precipitation	rain	condensation	ice

4. The earth uses the same water over and over again.

This is called the _____ cycle.

water	sun	fire	tree

On a separate piece of paper, draw a diagram to show the water cycle.

- The sun evaporates water from the earth.
- Water condenses and forms clouds.
- Precipitation falls from the clouds in the form of rain, snow, hail, or sleet.
- Water flows back to the lakes, rivers, and oceans.

Triangles are two dimensional shapes with three sides and three angles. There are different kinds of triangles.

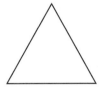

An equilateral triangle has three equal sides.

A right triangle must have one 90° angle and two angles that total exactly 90°.

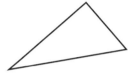

A scalene triangle has no equal sides or angles.

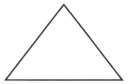

An isosceles triangle has at least two equal sides and angles.

1.	2. 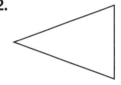	3.	4.
_____	_____	_____	_____
5. 	6. 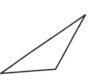	7.	8.
_____	_____	_____	_____

Choose your AEROBIC exercise!

Exercise for today:

_____

Check & Record in Fitness Log.

Day 4

KINDNESS

Kindness is being nice and caring about other people, animals and the earth. Kindness is looking for ways to understand and help others.

Value

PELE

Pele is from Brazil and is considered by many to be one of the best soccer players to ever play the game. At the age of 17, Pele scored two goals to help Brazil win the World Championship game. He entertained fans with his amazing plays and so many goals. It seemed that no one could keep him from scoring! Pele also had a big heart and a big smile. He loved to laugh and make other people feel good. He grew up poor and had to work hard doing whatever jobs he could find to help support his family. He never forgot the lessons he learned or the people that were less fortunate than him. When he retired, Pele dedicated his life to helping others around the world, especially children.

1. Why was Pele admired around the world?

_____

_____

2. Look up the following words in the dictionary and write the definitions.

Humanitarian: _____

_____

Extraordinary: _____

_____

Value: KINDNESS

FAMILY ACTIVITIES

Choose one or more activities to do with your family or friends.

 Play "10 good things" with your friends or family. Pick a person and tell 10 nice things about them.

 Write notes to your neighbors thanking them for being good neighbors.

 Have a lemonade stand and donate the money you earn to a food bank or homeless shelter.

 Collect toys, books, and games you no longer play with and donate them.

Let's talk about it...

Children learn what they live, if they see you practicing random acts of kindness, they will want to do them too. Discuss things your family can do together to help others. Set aside some time to volunteer at a soup kitchen or homeless shelter. Remind your child that kindness begins with a smile and should be practiced at home too!

VALUES ARE A FAMILY AFFAIR

 Read more about **KINDNESS**

Bully on the Bus
By Carl W. Bosch

What a Wimp
By Carol Carrick

Fourth Grade Rats
By Jerry Spinelli

Choose a game or activity to play for 60 minutes as a family or with friends today!

Day 5

Choose a **Play** or **Exercise** Activity!

Summer Explorer

Discover New Things to Play and Do!

- Learn how to make paper airplanes.

- Host a board game night.

- Play charades.

- Use cardboard boxes to build an outdoor house, fort, train, or pirate ship.

- Play jump rope, marbles, or hopscotch.

- Use "junk" from around your house to create an art masterpiece.

- Make some puppets and put on a puppet show.

- Go through your toys and have a toy exchange or donate to charity.

- Fly a kite.

- Draw with sidewalk or paint with water on the cement.

- Create a new exercise or exercise routine.

- Organize a neighborhood garbage walk to pick up trash and clean up your neighborhood.

- Search for animal tracks. How many can you identify?

- Play in the sand. Build a sand castle.

- Play Frisbee.

- Write a letter to someone and mail it.

- Visit a local nature preserve.

- Make a robot or other creation out of items from your recycle bin.

- Paint a pet rock.

Recyclable Creations "Junk Monsters"

 Gather clean cans, bottles, and boxes from recycling bin.

 Use plastic lids, newspaper strips, nuts, screws, buttons, pipe cleaners, rubber bands to make faces, and arms and legs. Your parents will need to help you glue with a hot glue gun.

 Create monsters, robots, or your family members!

Summer Journal III

Write about your best friend, brother or sister.

3–4 • © Summer Fit Activities™

Table of Contents

The table of contents is found at the beginning of a book. The table of contents lists the chapters and the page on which they start.

Table of Contents

Rocks and Minerals

Chapter	Page
1. What are Rocks?	3
2. Sedimentary, Igneous, and Metamorphic rocks	6
3. What are Minerals?	9
4. Crystals	12
5. What are Fossils?	14
6. Rock Collecting	17
7. Rock and Mineral Identification Guide	20

Look at the table of contents above and answer the question below.

1. What would you read about in chapter 2? _____

2. What chapter would you read to learn about fossils?_____

3. Where would you learn about equipment for rock collecting? _____

4. What page is the identification guide on? _____

5. What page does the chapter on crystals begin on? _____

6. What is the shortest chapter? _____

Write the contraction for each set of words. Don't forget the apostrophe.

7. he will _____	8. can not _____	9. you are _____
10. I am _____	11. they have _____	12. she is _____
13. has not _____	14. we will _____	15. we are _____
16. is not _____	17. they are _____	18. will not _____

Write each fraction as a decimal.

1. **Ex.** 8/10 = 0.8

2. 7/10 = _____

3. 75/100 = _____

4. 9/10 = _____

5. 5/10 = _____

6. 3/10 = _____

7. 10/100 = _____

8. 90/100 = _____

Write each decimal as a fraction.

9. **Ex.** .25 = 25/100 = 1/4

10. 0.6 = _____

11. 0.2 = _____

12. 0.5 = _____

13. 0.4 = _____

14. 0.75 = _____

15. 0.4 = _____

16. 0.9 = _____

17. 0.15 = _____

18. 0.35 = _____

The numerator is the top number of a fraction and tells how many equal parts are used. The denominator is the bottom number and tells how many equal parts in all.

$$\frac{1}{2} \quad \begin{array}{l} = \text{numerator} \\ = \text{denominator} \end{array}$$

Look at the fractions in each pair. Circle the fraction with the greater value.

19.   1/5   or   1/6

20.   1/2   or   1/4

21.   1/3   or   2/3

22.   4/5   or   1/5

23.   1/100   or   1/10

24.   1/7   or   4/7

Choose your AEROBIC exercise!

Exercise for today:

_____

Check & Record in Fitness Log.

Day 6

3-4 • © Summer Fit Activities™

Read the passage on bats then answer the questions below.

There are over a thousand different kinds of bats. Although they can be found all over the world, most of the world's bat population lives near the equator because of the warm climate. The largest bat has a wingspan of almost six feet, while the smallest bat is about as big as a bumblebee with just a five-inch wingspan. A bat's wingspan is the measurement from the tip of one wing to the tip of the other while fully extended.

Most bats are brown, but they can also be other colors, like black, white, red, and even yellow. Bats like to live in colonies with many other bats. They make their homes in caves, trees, tunnels, and attics. Bats are nocturnal, which means they are active at night and sleep during the day. While sleeping, bats hang upside down by their toes with their wings wrapped around them for protection.

Bats are mammals and feed their young with milk. Even though they can fly, bats are not birds. However, they are the only mammal that can fly like a bird. Bats have extremely good hearing and use a kind of sonar called echolocation to navigate the dark and hunt for food. Most bats eat insects, but some also eat rodents, fish, fruit, and even other bats. The famous vampire bat feed on the blood of cattle and birds. Because bats eat so many insects they are very important to the environment and help keep the insect population under control.

Write T if the statement is true and F if it is false. Correct the false statements.

1. Bats prefer a warmer climate. _____

2. Bats are nocturnal. _____

3. Most bats like to live alone. _____

4. Bats can be many different colors. _____

5. Bats are birds. _____

6. Bats are mammals. _____

7. Bats use their eyes to see in the dark. _____

8. Most bats don't eat insects. _____

9. The vampire bat feed on the blood of cattle and birds. _____

Divide.

1. How many 2's in 12? ___6___

2. How many 8's in 64? _____

3. How many 6's in 54? _____

4. How many 12's in 36? _____

5. How many 5's in 60? _____

6. How many 4's in 40? _____

7. How many 3's in 27? _____

8. How many 7's in 28? _____

Write the numbers in order from least to greatest.

9. 806   860   680   86   _____, _____, _____, _____.

10. 456   540   154   654   _____, _____, _____, _____.

11. 87   78   107   70   _____, _____, _____, _____.

12. 555   505   450   105   _____, _____, _____, _____.

Find the pattern and continue each row.

13. 68, 65, 62, _____, _____, _____, _____, _____ .

14. 7, 14, 21, _____, _____, _____, _____, _____ .

15. 80, 78, 76, _____, _____, _____, _____, _____ .

16. 115, 120, 125, _____, _____, _____, _____, _____ .

17. 200, 190, 180, _____, _____, _____, _____, _____ .

18. 56, 58, 60, _____, _____, _____, _____, _____ .

Add 100 to each number.

19. 32 _____   3, 270 _____   250 _____   24 _____

20. 576 _____   5,234 _____   345 _____   1,607 _____

Subtract 100 from each number.

21. 789 _____   198 _____   560 _____   351 _____

22. 2,560 _____   1,893 _____   2,990 _____   330 _____

Choose your STRENGTH exercise!

Exercise for today:

_____

Check & Record in Fitness Log.

Day 7

70

 **Adjectives and Adverbs**

Day 8

An adjective describes a noun. An adverb describes a verb. While many adverbs end in ly many adjectives do too.

Circle each -ly word and say whether it is an adjective or an adverb.

1. The children waited patiently in line for the movie. _____

2. The sleepy baby cried loudly on his mother's lap. _____

3. The sun shone brightly in the sky. _____

4. The farmer worked tirelessly plowing the fields. _____

5. The girl's curly hair bounced as she ran. _____

6. The smelly garbage sat in the can for days. _____

7. The soldiers fought bravely for their country. _____

8. The wind gently rustled the leaves in the trees. _____

9. The friendly clerk offered to help carry our packages. _____

10. We ran quickly to the car to get out of the rain. _____

Circle the adjective in each sentence and write the noun it modifies on the line.

Ex. The (giant) pumpkin was rolled onto the truck. <u>pumpkin</u>_____

11. The beautiful ballerina danced across the stage. _____

12. The shy boy shrugged his shoulders. _____

13. We picked a pretty bouquet of flowers for our grandma. _____

14. The fluffy kitten jumped onto my lap. _____

15. The marching band played three songs at the game. _____

16. The patient librarian read the book to a large group of toddlers. _____

Use an adjective and an adverb to complete each sentence.

Ex. The ___green___ snake slithered slowly behind the rock.

17. The _____ man walked _____ through the park.

18. The _____ spider skittered _____ up the wall.

19. The _____ band played _____ at the concert.

20. The _____ children _____ opened their presents.

Compare the Numbers

Write > ,<, or = for each pair.

1. **Ex.** 3 x 6 _>_ 10 + 4

2. $3.56 _____ $3.65

3. 7 x 6 _____ 9 x 5

4. 6 in. _____ 6 ft.

5. 3 + 4 _____ 3 x 4

6. 42 ÷ 7 _____ 36 ÷ 9

7. 40 ÷5 _____ 3 x 4

8. 4 x 4 _____ 2 x 8

9. 20 ÷ 4 _____ 9 - 3

10. 1 x 0 _____ 1 x 1

11. 5,020 _____ 5,202

12. 10 ÷5 _____ 20 ÷ 10

13. 1/2 _____ 1/4

14. .50 _____ 1/2

15. 9 x 11 _____ 100 - 10

16. 8 x 9 _____ 9 x 8

Fill in the blank with the best measurement, feet, inches, yards, centimeters, or miles.

17. The bookcase is 2 _____ deep.

18. Joseph's dad is 6 _____ tall.

19. The football field is 100 _____ long.

20. The library is 5 _____ from the house.

21. The pencil is 4 _____ long.

22. The bug is 2 _____ long.

Circle the greater of each pair.

23.	quart	cup
24.	inch	centimeter
25.	mile	yard
26.	day	week

27.	minute	second
28.	ounce	pound
29.	yard	foot
30.	dime	nickel

Choose your AEROBIC exercise!

Exercise for today:

_____

Day 8

Check & Record in Fitness Log.

3-4 • © Summer Fit Activities™

Subject and Predicates

All good sentences have a subject and a predicate. The subject of a sentence tells who or what the sentence is about. The predicate modifies or tells about the subject. The subject and predicate can be just one word or more than one word.

Circle the subject of each sentence and underline the predicate.

Ex. The (energetic monkeys) howled in the trees.

1. The big spider built a web under the porch.

2. Amanda and Rachel visited the Doll and Toy Museum.

3. The space alien landed his ship in the field.

4. Joe and his brother played in the chess tournament.

5. The children played in the sandbox.

6. The moon and stars shone brightly in the sky.

7. The horse galloped across the field.

8. We rode the bus to the zoo.

Write two complete sentences. Be sure to include the subject and the predicate.

9. _____

_____

_____.

10. _____

_____

_____.

The boiling point of water is 212° Fahrenheit or 100° Celsius

The freezing point of water is 32° Fahrenheit or 0° Celsius

Read each thermometer and write the temperature.

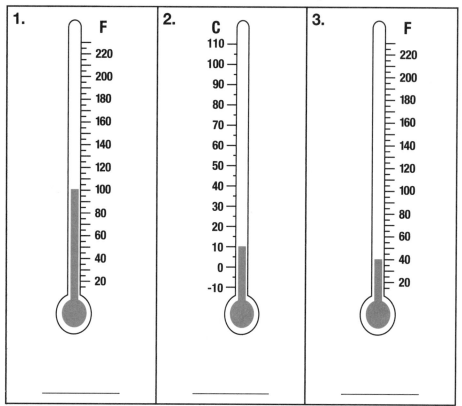

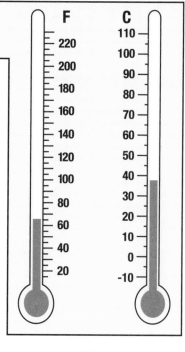

1.
2.
3.

_____   _____   _____

4. The boiling point of water is _____ ° Fahrenheit.

5. The freezing point of water is _____ ° Celsius.

6. The instrument used to measure temperature is called

a _____.

7. Color the thermometer to the right to show the temperature 64° F.

 Choose your STRENGTH exercise!

 **Day 9**

Exercise for today:

_____

Check & Record in Fitness Log.

COURAGE

Courage means doing the right thing even when it is difficult and you are afraid. It means to be brave.

Value

An Act of Courage

Rosa Parks had always dreamed things would be different. She dreamed of a day when there would be freedom for everyone and one day she stood up for everything she believed in. On that day in early December, 1955, Rosa got on the bus and instead of sitting in the back where the black people were supposed to sit, she sat in the front of the bus. The front of the bus was only reserved for white people and when the bus driver asked her to get up, Rosa refused. The police came and Rosa was arrested. Her courage made other people want to fight for freedom too and there was a boycott. The boycott meant that no black people rode the busses. Finally, the rules for riding the bus were changed and black and white people could sit wherever they wanted. Rosa is a hero because she stood up for what was right even though it was hard and even though she stood alone. Her act of courage helped other people want to stand up for what was right too.

Design an American postage stamp that shows why Rosa Parks is a hero. Color your stamp.

Value: COURAGE

FAMILY ACTIVITIES

Choose one or more activities to do with your family or friends.

 As a family, watch a movie that demonstrates courage such as *Charlotte's Web*, *The Sound of Music*, *The Wizard of Oz*, *The Lion King*, *ET*, or *Finding Nemo*. Discuss how the characters in the movie display courage. What might have happened if they hadn't been courageous?

 Make and decorate a pennant for your room that says "I believe in myself." Discuss with your parents how being the best you can be is an act of courage.

 Talk about the courage it takes for a blind person to get through the day. Take turns blindfolding each other and try to do your everyday things. Ask your parents to help you look up the story of Ben Underwood, a blind teen who rides a skateboard and plays video games.

 Think about the most courageous person you know. Write about how they demonstrate courage.

Let's talk about it...

Courage is something built over time. Discuss everyday situations with your child and the opportunities they have to be brave. Read books about people who display courage. Encourage them to share their fears and brainstorm together ways to face and overcome those fears. Talk with them about a time you were afraid but found the courage to get through.

VALUES ARE A FAMILY AFFAIR

Read more about COURAGE

Call It Courage
By Armstrong Sperry

Little House Books
By Laura Ingalls Wilder

The Castle in the Attic
By Elizabeth Winthrop

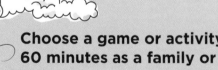

Choose a game or activity to play for 60 minutes as a family or with friends today!

Day 10
Choose a **Play** or **Exercise** Activity!

3–4 • © Summer Fit Activities™

INCENTIVE CONTRACT CALENDAR

My parents and I agree that if I complete this section of

Summer Fit Activities™

and read _____ minutes a day, my reward will be _____

Child Signature: _____   Parent Signature: _____

Day 1			Day 6		
Day 2			Day 7		
Day 3			Day 8		
Day 4			Day 9		
Day 5			Day 10		

Color the for each day of activities completed.

Color the for each day of reading completed.

3-4 • © Summer Fit Activities™

Summer Fitness Log

Choose your exercise activity each day from the Aerobic and Strength Activities in the back of the book. Record the date, stretch, activity and how long you performed your exercise activity below. Fill in how many days you complete your fitness activity on your Incentive Contract Calendars.

	Date	Stretch	Activity	Time
examples:	June 4	Run in place	Sky Reach	7 min
	June 5	Toe Touches	Bottle Curls	15 min
1.				
2.				
3.				
4.				
5.				
6.				
7.				
8.				
9.				
10.				

I promise to do my best for me. I exercise to be healthy and active. I am awesome because I am me.

Child Signature: _____

Eating healthy foods allows your body to get the nutrients it needs to function and grow. Making healthy choices and eating a balanced diet help give you the energy you need to learn, work, and play. Protein like beans and lean meats help your muscles grow and stay strong. Grains like bread, pasta and cereal are an important source of fiber that helps you digest your food and give you energy. Dairy products such as milk and cheese provide calcium for strong bones and teeth. Fruits and vegetables are all natural and are loaded with the vitamins and minerals your body needs. While sweets and fatty foods such as cake and french fries may taste good, they should be eaten only once in a while and in small amounts. These foods are high in calories and have no nutritional value.

Study the image from ChooseMyPlate.gov, then think of foods that fit into each category and write them in the correct column. An example of each has been done for you.

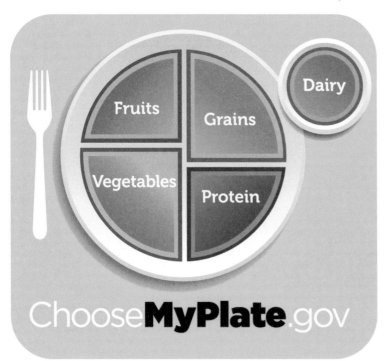

Tips for healthy eating:

- Drink a full glass of water at every meal and throughout the day.

- Choose fruits and vegetables for snacks.

- Ask your mom or dad if you can help plan healthy meals for the week, shop with them for healthy foods, and help prepare the healthy meals.

- Try to eat dinner as a family at least 3 times a week, at the table and with the tv off.

Write three examples of each kind of food.

protein	dairy	fruits	vegetables	grains	sweets
peanut butter	milk	peach	broccoli	oatmeal	cake

Round each amount to the nearest dollars.

Ex. $1.20 = $1.00

1. $.85 = _____ $1.00 _____

2. $1.76 = _____

3. $1.56 = _____

4. $19.59 = _____

5. $13.45 = _____

6. $ 5.98 = _____

7. $9.43 = _____

8. $12.77 = _____

9. $16.21 = _____

10. $8.09 = _____

How much money?

11.	2 quarters	_____._____	12.	3 quarters	_____._____
	3 nickels	_____._____		12 dimes	_____._____
	23 pennies	+ _____._____		4 nickels	+ _____._____
		$ _____._____			$ _____._____

Add or subtract to find the answer.

13. $24.00
  + $17.50

14. $85.00
  - $36.25

15. $23.86
  + $14.72

16. $260.38
  - $158.24

17. $ 83.50
  x 2

18. $24.54
  x 5

Choose your STRENGTH exercise!

Exercise for today:

_____

Check & Record in Fitness Log.

Day 1

 **Simile**

A **simile** is a comparison made between two unlike things. The word simile comes from a Latin word that means sameness. **Similes** can make our writing and speaking more interesting. We can easily recognize a **simile** because it will use the words " like" or "as". For example: "as soft as a marshmallow" or "runs like the wind."

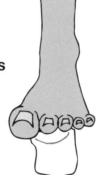

Match each phrase on the left with a phrase on the right to complete a simile.

1. As big as a...	baby
2. As cute as a...	old shoe
3. They fought like...	button
4. As hard as a...	hyena
5. I slept like a...	rock
6. As flat as a...	glove
7. It fits like a...	house
8. He laughs like a...	pancake
9. As comfortable as an...	cats and dogs

Choose 3 of the phrases from the first column and make up your own comparison for the second phrase.

10. _____

11. _____

12. _____

Sam's basketball team scored the following points for their June games. What was the average score?

5, 7, 9, 7, 10, 8, 10

Ex. 5 + 7 + 9 + 7+ 10 + 8 +10 = 56   56 ÷ 7 = 8 Average score = 8

Use addition and division to find the averages.

1. 1 + 4 + 2 + 7 + 3 + 8 + 2 + 5 = _____

2. 8 + 3 + 6 + 3 + 8 + 2 + 8 + 2 = _____

3. 7 + 5 + 9 + 7 + 2 + 4 + 8 + 6 = _____

4. 6 + 3 + 7 + 4 + 5 + 4 + 6 = _____

5. 3 + 8 + 6 + 7 + 5 + 9 + 4 = _____

6. Daniel bought an apple for .50 cents. He paid with a dollar.

How much change did he get back? _____

7. Emma bought a cookie for .75 cents. She paid with a dollar.

How much change did she get back._____

Solve and check.

8. x + 6 = 10 + 5 -1   x = _____   9. x - 4 = 12 ÷ 3   x = _____

Work the problems. Solve within the parentheses first and pay attention to the signs.

10. 2 x (42 ÷ 7) + 8 = _____   11. 9 x (2 + 3) - 4 = _____

12. 16 – (3 x 3) + 6 = _____   13. 5 + (6 x 2) – 3 = _____

Choose your AEROBIC exercise!

Exercise for today:

_____

Day 2

Check & Record in Fitness Log.

Here is a map of the United States of America. Use a globe or an atlas to answer the questions below.

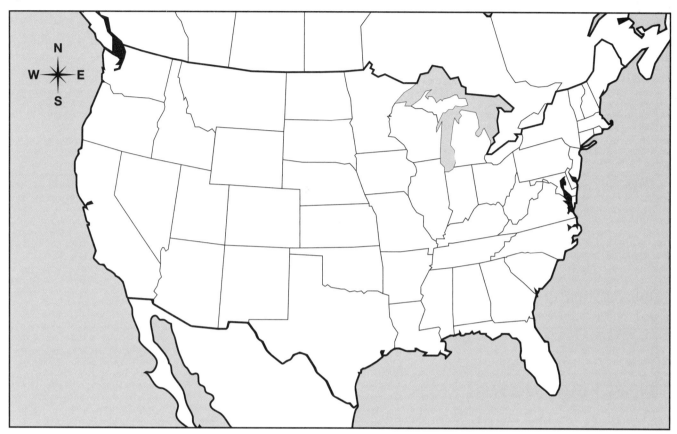

1. Find and label the Pacific and Atlantic Oceans.

2. Find and label the following states: California, Florida, Washington, Minnesota, Pennsylvania, Utah, and Arizona.

3. Find and label the U.S. capital.

4. Label the largest and smallest states.

4. Find and label your state and your state's capital.

5. Label the state east of Alabama.

6. Find and label the Dakotas and the Carolinas.

7. Find and locate the state with the capital Lincoln.

8. Find and label USA's neighboring countries.

Write the digits in the proper places. Read the numbers.

	Thousands	Hundreds	Tens	Ones
Ex. **543**		5	4	3
1. 987	_____	_____	_____	_____
2. 1,276	_____	_____	_____	_____
3. 5,820	_____	_____	_____	_____
4. 694	_____	_____	_____	_____
5. 9,041	_____	_____	_____	_____
6. 8,349	_____	_____	_____	_____

Show 6 x 3 = 18 four ways.

7. _____ 9. _____

8. _____ 10. _____

Show 8 x 4 = 32 four ways.

11. _____ 13. _____

12. _____ 14. _____

15. What time is it?   16. What time was it 25 minutes ago?

_____:_____   _____:_____

Choose your STRENGTH exercise!

Exercise for today:

_____

Day 3

Letters and Sounds - Circle the letter of the beginning sound.

 **Day 4**

The verb "be" tells what the subject of a sentence <u>is</u> or <u>was</u>. "Am," "is," and "are" tell about the subject in the <u>present</u>. "Was" and "were" tell about the subject in the <u>past</u>.

Write the form of "be" to complete each sentence.

were	are	is	was	am

1. The beach _____ a fun place to go.

2. Sand castles _____ fun to build in the sand.

3. There _____ many families at the beach last weekend.

4. My surfboard _____ a gift from my parents.

5. I _____ training to be a junior lifeguard.

Circle the verb that best completes the sentence.

6. I (is, am) nine years old.

7. Mary and Beth (are, is) best friends.

8. The dogs (was, were) barking loudly when the doorbell rang.

9. We (are, is) going to plant a garden this summer.

10. My Grandma (is, are) coming for a visit.

Geometry

Classify each set of lines as intersecting, parallel, or perpendicular.

1.

_____

2.

_____

3.

_____

4.

_____

5.

_____

6.

_____

How many lines of symmetry in each shape?

7.

M

_____

8.

H

_____

9.

T

_____

10.

 I

_____

11.

A

_____

12.

X

_____

Choose your AEROBIC exercise!

Exercise for today:

Check & Record in Fitness Log.

Day 4

3-4 • © Summer Fit Activities™

SummerFitActivities.com

RESPECT

Value

*Respect is honoring
yourself and others.*

RESPECT

Mahatma Gandhi was a great political and spiritual leader of India. His name means "Great Soul" and although he was meek and humble, he demonstrated that true strength came from peace and harmony. For years he helped people stand up against unfair treatment. His "weapons" were peaceful protests, marches, and strikes. Gandhi believed that every life was valuable and worthy of respect and he worked hard to protect the rights of all people. He lived what he preached and his life was an example of how to live in peace and harmony. Gandhi taught that if you hurt another person you were really hurting yourself. He wanted people to find peaceful ways of reconciling their differences and to live in harmony with love and respect for all, even their enemies.

Antonyms are words that mean the opposite. Choose an antonym from the list to fill in each blank.

war	lose	help	weakness	worthless	arrogant

1. valuable _____

2. strength _____

3. gain _____

4. humble _____

5. peace _____

6. hurt _____

7. What lesson did Gandhi teach?

_____

_____

Value: RESPECT

Respect is showing good manners and acceptance of other people and our planet. Respect is celebrating differences in culture, ideas and experiences that are different than yours. Respect is accepting that others have lessons to teach us because of their experiences.

"Be the change you want to see in the world."

- Mahatma Gandhi

List 3 ways to show respect to your parents and teachers.

1 _____

2 _____

3 _____

We can disrespect people with our words. Remember to THINK before we speak. Ask yourself...

T = is it true?

H = Is it helpful or hurtful?

I = Is it inspiring?

N = Is it necessary?

K = Is it kind?

WAYS TO SHOW RESPECT

Respect the Earth.
Collect items to recycle.

Respect a different culture:
Listen to some music or try a new food that is associated with a culture or belief that is different than yours.

Day 5 Choose a **Play** or **Exercise** Activity!

Summer Explorer
Discover New Things to Play and Do!

- Learn the phases of the moon. Look at it several nights in a row and see if you can recognize the various phases.

- Make up a song or dance.

- Have a yard sale.

- Start a rock collection.

- Have a potluck with family and friends.

- Visit a farmers market. Learn about the origin of the food you eat.

- Volunteer.

- Take a hike.

- Have a neighborhood softball game.

- Make popsicles.

- Grab some binoculars and go on a bird watching hike.

- Go camping.

- Have a western theme night. Wear bandannas and your cowboy boots, and roast hotdogs. Try line dancing or watch an old Western.

- Go on a nature walk. Collect twigs, leaves, pebbles, and shells. Glue them on card stock to make a 3D masterpiece.

- Help a neighbor by mowing their lawn or weeding.

- Draw a comic strip.

- Bake cookies and take some to a friend or neighbor.

- Play Hide and Seek.

- Have a pillow fight.

- Create a time capsule.

Nature Walk

 Go on a nature walk in a field, park or beach.

 Collect grass, twigs, shells, pebbles, etc.

 Arrange your finds inside a cardboard box, glue down to create a 3D masterpiece.

Summer Journal IV

Write about your best summer day so far.

Jacques Cousteau (1910-1997) was the world's most famous oceanographer. Cousteau combined his two loves: the ocean and film-making to bring the underwater world to millions of people. He was also a great writer and inventor. Look in an encyclopedia or on the internet to find out more about this fascinating man.

Oceans

Oceans make up more than 70% of our planet's surface and contain over 90% of the earth's water. People everywhere depend on the ocean for food and energy. There are five oceans in the world. From largest to smallest they are the Pacific Ocean, Atlantic Ocean, Indian Ocean, Southern Ocean, and Arctic Ocean. The Pacific Ocean covers nearly 1/3 of the earth's surface and is larger than the seven continents put together.

Oceanography is the study of the ocean and all that it contains. Oceanographers explore and study the ocean and all that it contains. Oceanographers explore and study the ocean to learn about its environment and all its inhabitants, plant and animal. Oceanographers use many tools to help them learn about the ocean, including satellites, submersibles, sonar devices, and current meters. With all the equipment available to them, oceanographers can study and chart parts of the ocean never explored before.

Answer the questions.

1. The oceans contain what percentage of the earth's water?

2. Name the world's five oceans from smallest to largest. _____,

_____, _____, _____, _____.

3. What is an oceanographer? _____

Look up the word <u>submersible</u> in the dictionary and write the definition.

_____

_____

Look on a globe or map to find the earth's five oceans. How quickly can you locate them?

Look at the graph showing the number of cans Mr. Dean's 4th grade class collected over the school year.

Cans collected September through May

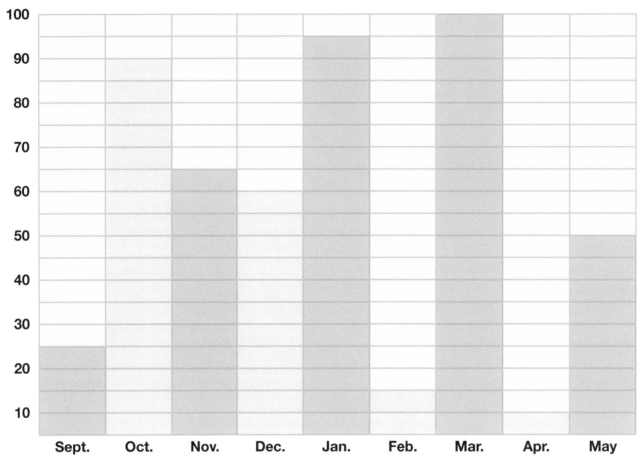

1. During which month were the most cans collected? _____

2. During which month were the fewest cans collected? _____

3. What is the average of the number of cans collected during September, October, and November? _____

4. How many more cans were collected in March than in April? _____

5. Write the amount of cans collected from least to greatest. _____

_____

6. What is the range of the cans collected (difference between most and least)? _____

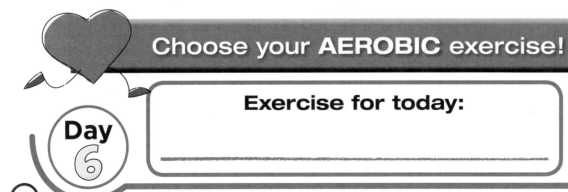

Choose your AEROBIC exercise!

Exercise for today:

_____

Day 6

Check & Record in Fitness Log.

3-4 • © Summer Fit Activities™

Verbs: past, present, and future

Complete the sentences using verbs from the verb box.

Fill in the verbs using the past tense.

1. Last week I _____ the lawn.

2. Yesterday, I _____ pancakes for breakfast.

3. We _____ marshmallows before we put out the campfire.

4. The baby birds _____ in their nest.

VERB BOX
mow
eat
toast
chirp

Fill in the verbs using present tense.

5. When the kettle _____, will you make some tea?

6. The baby is _____ with the toy.

7. Mom is _____ dinner in the kitchen.

8. Grandma is _____ me a sweater.

VERB BOX
boil
play
cook
make

Fill in the verbs using future tense.

9. Tim _____ _____ tomorrow when he gets home.

10. I _____ _____ the ball next time .

11. The eggs _____ _____ in about 21 days.

12. I _____ _____ the piano every day.

VERB BOX
skate
catch
hatch
practice

Time Problems. Use the hands on the clocks to answer the following questions.

1.

What time was it 45 minutes ago? _____

What time will it be in 1 hour? _____

How many minutes until 9:45? _____

2.

What time will it be in 20 minutes? _____

What time was it 30 minutes ago? _____

How many minutes until 3:55? _____

3.

What time was it 45 minutes ago? _____

What time will it be in 35 minutes? _____

How many minutes until 1:00? _____

4. One play ticket costs $12.00. How much will Jacob need to buy 4 tickets?

$ _____

5. Noah bought a book for $6.87 and paid with a $10.00 bill.

How much change did he get back? $ _____ Draw the change.

Frankie could buy 4 cookies for $2.00 or 8 cookies for $3.00. Circle the better buy.

4 cookies	8 cookies

Choose your STRENGTH exercise!

Exercise for today:

_____

Day 7

Check & Record in Fitness Log.

Look it up

Guide words appear at the top of each dictionary page and are in alphabetical order. The word on the top left is the first word on the page. The word on the top right is the last word on the page.

The guide words on a dictionary page are *fireworks* and *fishing*. Circle all the words words you would find on that page.

Fireworks	Fishing
firm	frame
fight	first
fish	fisherman
fishhook	fast

Number each set of words in alphabetical order

1.

snake _____

silly _____

snow _____

shovel _____

second _____

2.

hammer _____

happy _____

hare _____

heavy _____

hedge _____

3.

owl _____

order _____

open _____

odor _____

office _____

4.

dance _____

dishes _____

danger _____

door _____

direct _____

Menu Math

Read and answer the story problems using the menu.

MENU

Hot dog $1.25	Soda $1.00	Fries .85
Hamburger $2.00	Salad $3.00	Ice Cream $1.50

1. Sophie ordered a hot dog, fries, and a soda. How much did her order cost?_____

2. Sophie paid with $5.00. How much was her change?_____

3. Jack ordered a hamburger, salad, and ice cream. How much did his food cost? _____

4. Jack paid with a $10 bill. How much change did he get back?_____

5. Kim wants to order a salad, fries, and ice cream. If she has only $5.00, will she have

   enough money? _____. If not, how much more will she need?

6. What is the most expensive item on the menu?_____

7. What is the least expensive item on the menu?_____

8. How much would two hamburgers, two orders of fries, and one ice cream cost? _____

Choose your AEROBIC exercise!

Exercise for today:

Check & Record in Fitness Log.

Think of a person, living or dead, who is your hero. Write their name in the center of the web above "My Hero." Fill in the other bubbles with adjectives to describe your hero.

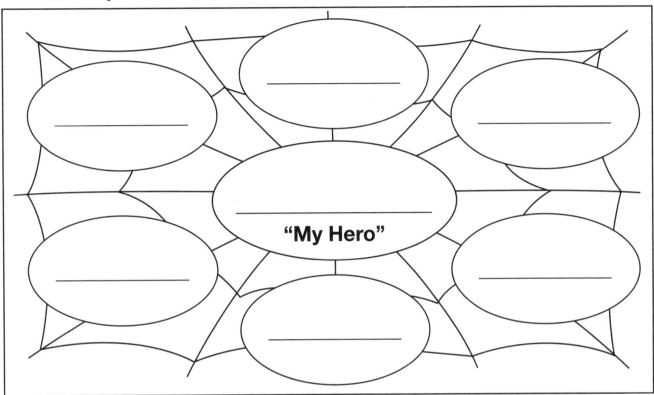

Write a paragraph on your hero. Remember to include a topic sentence, supporting sentences, and a conclusion. Use your best handwriting and watch your spelling and punctuation. Write the title on the top line.

_____

_____

_____

_____

_____

_____

Topic Sentence tells the main idea of the paragraph.
Supporting Sentences give detail about the main idea.
Concluding Sentences sum up the paragraph or give a final thought to bring it to a clear end.

To find the area of each rectangle, multiply the length by the width. Write the area on each line.

1.

4 in

3 in

Area = _____ in ^{2}

4.

12 ft

4 ft

Area = _____ ^{2} ft

2.

7 cm

5 cm

Area = _____ ^{2} cm

5.

10 m

5 m

Area = _____ ^{2} m

3.

9 ft

8 ft

Area = _____ ^{2} ft

6.

8 in

4 in

Area = _____ in ^{2}

Choose your STRENGTH exercise!

Day 9

Exercise for today:

_____

Check & Record in Fitness Log.

3-4 • © Summer Fit Activities™

Value

Responsibility is to do what you think you should, for yourself and others, even when it is difficult.

Terrance Stanley Fox was a very good athlete. His favorite sport was basketball but he also played rugby, golf and ran cross country in high school. Sadly, Terry lost one of his legs because he got cancer. He felt it was his responsibility to do all that he could for other people with cancer and even though it was very hard, he set off to run across Canada with an artificial leg to raise money for cancer research. He called his run the Marathon of Hope. When he started to run not many people knew about Terry or what he was doing but now people all over the world participate or take part in the event. The annual Terry Fox Run has become the world's largest one-day fund raiser for cancer research.

When Terry Fox was diagnosed with cancer he could have given up, but instead he inspired us and gave others hope.

Fill in the blanks with words from the story.

1. Terrance Stanley Fox was an athlete from _____ .

2. He had to have one of his legs amputated because of _____ .

3. Terrance felt it was his responsibility to raise money for _____ .

4. He ran across Canada with an artificial leg to raise _____ .

5. Terrance called his marathon the Marathon of _____ .

6. Look up the word amputate in the dictionary and write down its meaning.

amputate: _____

_____

Value: RESPONSIBILITY

You can show responsibility in many different ways. From doing your homework to babysitting your little brother or sister to helping someone else who is in need, being responsible is being accountable for your actions. Big and small, choosing what you do with your time and efforts is an important part of being responsible.

> "I am not doing the run to become rich or famous."
>
> - Terry Fox, *Marathon of Hope*

Monday	
Tuesday	
Wednesday	
Thursday	
Friday	
Saturday	
Sunday	

Build or set up a bird feeder in your yard and be responsible for feeding the birds. Use the chart below to track how many birds you feed for a week.

We are all responsible for the environment. Watch one of these family movies and talk about how being irresponsible can affect the environment. Movies: *Over the Hedge, Hoot, Free Willy, Bambi, Fern Gully, The Last Rainforest*, or *Happy Feet*.

Day 10 — Choose a **Play** or **Exercise** Activity!

INCENTIVE CONTRACT CALENDAR

My parents and I agree that if I complete this section of

Summer Fit Activities™

and read _____ minutes a day, my reward will be _____

Child Signature: _____   Parent Signature: _____

Day 1			Day 6		
Day 2			Day 7		
Day 3			Day 8		
Day 4			Day 9		
Day 5			Day 10		

Color the for each day of activities completed.

Color the for each day of reading completed.

Summer Fitness Log

Choose your exercise activity each day from the Aerobic and Strength Activities in the back of the book. Record the date, stretch, activity and how long you performed your exercise activity below. Fill in how many days you complete your fitness activity on your Incentive Contract Calendars.

	Date	Stretch	Activity	Time
examples:	June 4	Run in place	Sky Reach	7 min
	June 5	Toe Touches	Bottle Curls	15 min
1.				
2.				
3.				
4.				
5.				
6.				
7.				
8.				
9.				
10.				

I promise to do my best for me. I exercise to be healthy and active. I am awesome because I am me.

Child Signature: _____

 **Explosive Endings**

 **Day 1**

Look at the word ending in each rocket.

WORD BANK

slow	mix	sing	teach	work
fast	swim	play	fix	strong
short	long	black	rich	great

ing

ed

er

est

Use words from the word bank to make as many new words as you can .

teacher _____   _____   _____

teaching _____   _____   _____

_____   _____   _____

_____   _____   _____

_____   _____   _____

_____   _____   _____

_____   _____   _____

Add or subtract these fractions with like denominators.

1. $\dfrac{2}{3} + \dfrac{5}{3} =$

2. $\dfrac{2}{4} + \dfrac{5}{4} =$

3. $\dfrac{3}{7} + \dfrac{2}{7} =$

4. $\dfrac{1}{5} + \dfrac{3}{5} =$

5. $\dfrac{1}{4} + \dfrac{2}{4} =$

6. $\dfrac{3}{4} - \dfrac{2}{4} =$

7. $\dfrac{3}{7} + \dfrac{4}{7} =$

8. $\dfrac{4}{5} + \dfrac{2}{5} =$

9. $\dfrac{6}{9} + \dfrac{3}{9} =$

Compare the fractions and fill in greater than (>), less than (<), or equal to (=).

10. $\dfrac{1}{3}$ ____ $\dfrac{2}{3}$

11. $\dfrac{3}{4}$ ____ $\dfrac{1}{4}$

12. $\dfrac{1}{2}$ ____ $\dfrac{1}{4}$

13. $\dfrac{3}{4}$ ____ $\dfrac{1}{3}$

14. $\dfrac{1}{2}$ ____ $\dfrac{2}{4}$

15. $\dfrac{2}{4}$ ____ $\dfrac{3}{6}$

16. $\dfrac{1}{5}$ ____ $\dfrac{3}{5}$

17. $\dfrac{7}{10}$ ____ $\dfrac{8}{10}$

18. $\dfrac{6}{12}$ ____ $\dfrac{9}{12}$

Fill in the missing fractions on the number line.

19. $\dfrac{1}{9}$ $\dfrac{2}{9}$ ____ ____ ____ $\dfrac{6}{9}$ ____ $\dfrac{8}{9}$

 Choose your STRENGTH exercise!

Exercise for today:

_____

Check & Record in Fitness Log.

 **Sentence**

A sentence is a group of words that express a complete thought, while a sentence fragment is a group of words that expresses an incomplete thought. Write S if the word is a sentence and F if it is a fragment. If the group of words is a fragment, rewrite on the line as a complete sentence.

Ex. The flowers in the garden. __F__ The flowers in the garden were planted by my mother.

1. The fire truck raced loudly down the street. _____ _____

2. Build nests in trees. _____ _____

3. My favorite food is pizza. _____ _____

4. The dog didn't like _____ _____

5. Mom baked a cake. _____ _____

6. I like to. _____ _____

7. Shoe salesman. _____ _____

8. I will ride the bus to school. _____ _____

9. I wish I. _____ _____

10. My friends and I had a sleepover. _____ _____

11. The camping trip. _____ _____

12. Clean your room! _____ _____

Write the article "a" or "an" before each word.

Ex. _An_ elephant

13. _____ library

14. _____ igloo

15. _____ fly

16. _____ eagle

17. _____ ice cube

18. _____ bat

19. _____ ape

20. _____ tree

21. _____ egg

22. _____ kite

23. _____ ant

Use the number in the center of the wheel to multiply.

2.

1.

16

10

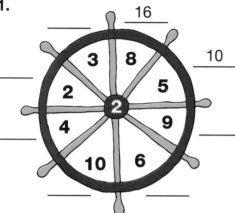

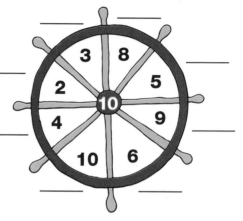

3.

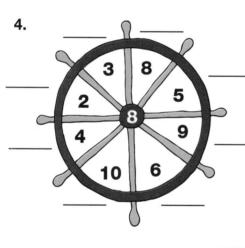

5.

4.

6.

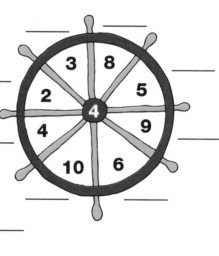

Choose your AEROBIC exercise!

Exercise for today:

Check & Record in Fitness Log.

Day 2

3-4 • © Summer Fit Activities™

SummerFitActivities.com

 **Ecosystems**

 **Day 3**

An ecosystem is all the living and non-living things in a certain area and how they interact with each other. Living things in an ecosystem are the animals, plants, and bacteria in a community. Non-living things are things like rocks, soil, water, and air. There are six different ecosystems in the world: ocean, desert, tundra, forest , grasslands, and wetlands.

Look at the four examples of ecosystems. Write the name of each ecosystem described below.

Make an ecosystem diorama. Use a shoebox and decorate the inside to look like the landscape of your chosen ecosystem. Find or make pictures of the plants and animals that live and interact there and glue or hang them in your box. Write a paragraph or poem describing your ecosystem.

1. This ecosystem is very wet with an abundance of fish and turtles. Other living things include alligators, toads, snakes, cattails, crayfish, raccoons, waterweed, and muskrat.

This ecosystem is a _____.

2. This ecosystem is very dry with hot days and cool nights. Some of the plants and animals that live here are cactus, coyote, scorpion, roadrunner, rattlesnake, and tortoise.

The name of this ecosystem is a _____.

3. The plant and animal dwellers in this salty environment are diverse and include sharks, whales, dolphins, coral reef, starfish, jellyfish, swordfish, seaweed, kelp, and phytoplankton.

The name of this ecosystem is the _____.

4.This ecosystem is warm and wet and full of trees. It has an intricate group of plants and animals that depend on heavy rainfall. Some of the many plants and animals that live there include the gorilla, sloth, howler monkey, chameleon, jaguar, capybara, anaconda, ferns, orchid, and toucan.

The name of this ecosystem is_____.

3-4 • © Summer Fit Activities™

Divide and check.

1. 3$\overline{)8{,}031}$ 2. 6$\overline{)2{,}748}$

Multiply.

3.	6,487	4.	4,320	5.	432	6.	621
	x 3		x 5		x 21		x 13

Continue each pattern using multiples of 10.

7. 10, 20, _____, _____, _____, 60	10. 800, 790, _____, _____, _____, 750
8. 150, 160, _____, _____, _____, 200	11. 1,210, 1,220, _____, _____, _____, 1,260
9. 340, 350, _____, _____, _____, 390	12. 5,670, 5,660, _____, _____, _____, 5,620

Solve quickly.

13. 8 x 4 = _____	16. 45 ÷ 5 = _____	19. 3 x 9 = _____	22. 36 ÷ 9 = _____
14. 6 x 6 = _____	17. 72 ÷ 9 = _____	20. 8 x 7 = _____	23. 9 x 4 = _____
15. 12 ÷ 2 = _____	18. 10 x 8 = _____	21. 28 ÷ 4 = _____	24. 3 x 7 = _____

Choose your STRENGTH exercise!

Exercise for today:

_____

Check & Record in Fitness Log.

Day 3

Write about your greatest summer adventure. Be sure to include colorful adjectives and interesting facts. Use correct punctuation, spelling, and write in your best handwriting. Draw a picture to go with your story.

_____

_____

_____

_____

_____

_____

_____

_____

_____

_____

_____

Draw the lines of symmetry on each shape. Each shape could have none, one, or more than one line of symmetry.

Ex.

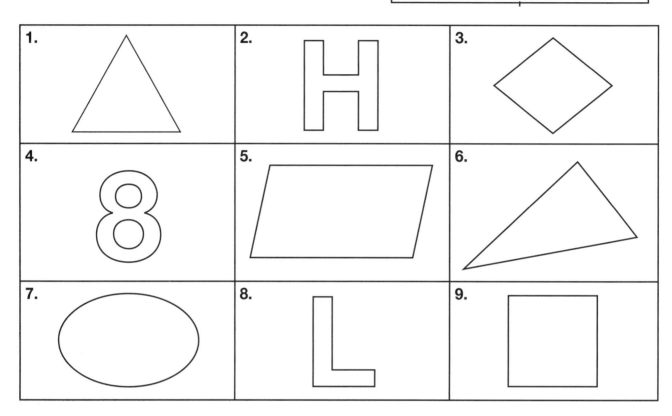

1.

2.

3.

4.

5.

6.

7.

8.

9.

Draw the other half of each object. The line of symmetry has been drawn for you.

10.

11.

12.

Choose your AEROBIC exercise!

Check & Record in Fitness Log.

Exercise for today:

Day 4

3-4 • © Summer Fit Activities™

PERSEVERANCE

Value

Perseverance is not giving up or giving in when things are difficult. It means you try again when you fail.

Shark Attack! **Bethany Hamilton** was sitting on her surfboard one sunny day in Hawaii, waiting for the next big wave. Suddenly a tiger shark attacked her and thirteen-year old Bethany lost one of her arms. Bethany survived and decided that she wanted to surf again. It wasn't easy because she had to overcome her fear of another shark attack and teach herself how to surf with only one arm. Little by little, she fought against the odds to succeed and was soon competing in and winning professional surfing competitions.

Bethany persevered and never gave up on her dreams. Rather than feel sorry for herself, she found a way to overcome her obstacles. Bethany decided that not only was she not going to give up on her dreams, but she wasn't going to let other kids give up on their dreams either. Bethany visited children in Thailand who had survived the Tsunami to help them get over their fears of getting in the water. She continues to travel around the world encouraging children with disabilities to follow their dreams no matter what. Bethany is proof that "where there is a will, there is a way."

Write a passage telling why Bethany Hamilton is a hero and how she has inspired you.

_____

_____

_____

_____

_____

_____

_____

Value: PERSEVERANCE

FAMILY ACTIVITIES

Choose one or more activities to do with your family or friends.

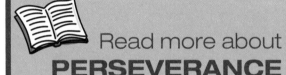

Let's talk about it...

Talk with your child about what perseverance is and why it's important. Discuss the importance of not giving up and sticking with something until it is complete. Lead by example and point out something you are involved in that is difficult and share with he/she how and why you are going to finish.

 As a family, tackle a big job you have been putting off such as cleaning the garage or painting the fence. Work together as a family to persevere and finish the job. Celebrate with ice cream to emphasize the sweet satisfaction of a job well done.

 People with disabilities face many obstacles each day. Read about Helen Keller and her perseverance in overcoming her blindness and deafness. Put on a blindfold and imagine how hard it would be to go about your day without your sight. What can you do? What can't you do?

 Farmers need perseverance and a lot of patience when planting their crops. One bad storm or drought can destroy everything they have worked for. Plant a small vegetable garden and take care of weeding and watering it. Be patient and your perseverance will pay off.

VALUES ARE A FAMILY AFFAIR

Read more about PERSEVERANCE

The Big Wave
By Pearl S. Buck

The Cay
By Theodore Taylor

Julie of the Wolves
By Jean Craighead George

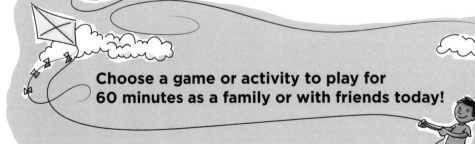

Choose a game or activity to play for 60 minutes as a family or with friends today!

Day 5

Choose a **Play** or **Exercise** Activity!

Summer Explorer

Discover New Things to Play and Do!

- Make up a secret handshake.

- Play "I spy".

- Write a poem.

- Make a telescope out of paper towel tubes. Have a family stargazing night: How many constellations can you find? Can you find the Big Dipper? Polaris?

- Do a puzzle.

- Make ice cream.

- Make a friendship bracelet and give it to a friend.

- Learn to fold Origami.

- Go fishing.

- Camp in the backyard.

- Learn how to juggle.

- Feed the ducks.

- Turn on some music and dance.

- Hang butcher paper on a wall and paint a mural.

- Learn the alphabet in sign language.

- Learn Pig Latin.

- Host a tea party.

- Have a Super Hero Day - dress like your favorite super hero or make up your own. Dress up your pet!

- Walk a dog.

- Do a science experiment.

- Pretend you are a reporter. Interview someone special and write an article about him/her.

Stargazing

 Collect paper towel tubes.

 Gather your family on a clear night to stargaze through your "telescopes".

 Look for The Big Dipper, Cancer and other star constellations.

3-4 • © Summer Fit Activities™

Summer Journal V

Write about your favorite pet or animal.

E-mail Book Report

Choose a book that is non-fiction and is an appropriate reading level for you. Pick a book that you are interested in and write the title and author here.

Book Title: _____

Author: _____

Illustrator: (if there is one) _____

Read the book.

Now think of someone you think would enjoy this book too. This person can be a friend or relative. Think about the book you just read. What information could you share with your friend to peak their interest and make them want to read this book? What do you think they might want to know about the characters, plot, setting, writing style, etc.? Remember to organize your thoughts, give specific examples but don't give away the ending! Use persuasive writing to really peak your friend or relative's interest.

Print out what you would write your friend here. If your parents give their permission, send the email to your friend.

To: _____

From: _____

Dear_____, I just read a great book called _____

_____. I think you would really like it because _____

_____

_____.

Let me tell you about it. _____

_____

_____

_____

_____

_____

_____

Fill in each blank with the appropriate measurement.

feet	inches	dozen	pounds	years	dollars
miles	yards	hour	minutes	gallon	ounces

1. Mom got a _____ donuts for my soccer team.

2. Dad is 6 _____ tall.

3. My dog weighs 40 _____.

4. I got a _____ of milk from the store.

5. I drank 16 _____ of soda.

6. The football field is 100 _____ long.

7. My grandpa is 65 _____ old.

8. The movie ticket cost five _____.

9. The next town is 45 _____ away.

10. The candy bar was 5 _____ long.

11. I read my book for 1 _____ last night.

12. I made my bed in 5 _____.

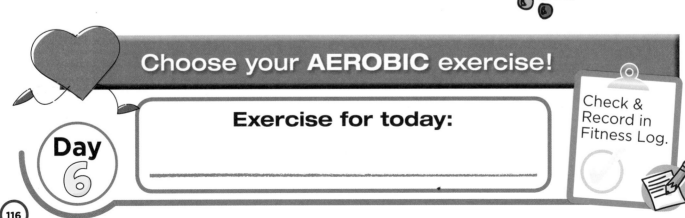

Choose your **AEROBIC** exercise!

Exercise for today:

Day 6

Check & Record in Fitness Log.

Third-Fourth Grade Spelling Words

Read these spelling words to a parent or guardian. Then copy them, in cursive, in your best handwriting.

reindeer _____   hymn _____

column _____   solemn _____

weigh _____   thumb _____

neighbor _____   photograph _____

once _____   chalk _____

knowledge _____   would _____

alligator _____   camera _____

handle _____   entertain _____

Use words from the list above to answer the questions.

1. The children drew on the sidewalk with _____.

2. Many fairy tales begin with the words "_____ upon a time."

3. Another word for picture is _____.

4. To _____ something is to find out how heavy or light it is.

5. An upright structure that looks like a post is called a _____.

6. A word that means to amuse or keep interested is _____.

7. The funeral was a very _____ affair.

8. When the man lifted the heavy suitcase, the _____ broke.

9. To have no understanding or awareness of something is to have no _____ of it.

10. We brought our _____ Mr. Long dinner after he returned home from his surgery.

3-4 • © Summer Fit Activities™

SummerFitActivities.com

117

A pictograph uses pictures or symbols to show data. Use the pictograph to answer the questions below.

Mrs. Brown's 4th grade class voted on their favorite fruit.

Each face represents two votes. **= 2 votes**

Apples:

Bananas :

Watermelon:

Oranges:

Pineapple:

1. How many children like bananas most? _____

2. How many more children like watermelon than oranges? _____

3. What is the classes favorite fruit? _____

4. How many more children like apples than bananas? _____

5. What is the classes least favorite fruit? _____

6. How many children from Mrs. Brown's class voted? _____

 ## Choose your STRENGTH exercise!

Exercise for today:

 **Day 7**

_____

 Check & Record in Fitness Log.

Landforms

The Earth is full of many different landforms. Draw a line from each picture to the name and description of its landform.

1.

2.

3.

4.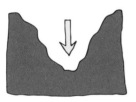

5.

6.

7.

Island: land completely surrounded by water.

Plain: open, flat land.

Peninsula: land surrounded by water on three sides.

Valley: area of low land that is between mountains and hills.

Plateau: high, level, flat land

Volcano: mountain or hill made from melted rock.

Mountain: high land mass with steep sides.

Hill: slightly raised area of land.

Calendar Days

Write the abbreviation for each month's name. The number of days is in parenthesis.

1. January (31) _____

2. October (31) _____

3. August (31) _____

4. June (30) _____

5. April (30) _____

6. February (28 or 29) _____

7. November (30) _____

8. September (30) _____

9. July (31) _____

10. May (31) _____

11. March (31) _____

12. December (31) _____

Fill in the blanks.

13. 1 Year = _____ months.

14. 1 week has _____ days.

15. 1 year = _____ days unless it is a leap year then it has _____ days.

16. 1 year has 52 _____.

Sunday	Monday	Tuesday	Wednesday	Thursday	Friday	Saturday
		1	2	3	4	5
6	7	8	9	10	11	12
13	14	15	16	17	18	19
20	21	22	23	24	25	26
27	28					

17. What is the name of this month? _____

18. Circle all the Mondays. How many are there in this month? _____

19. According to this calendar is this a leap year? _____

20. If this was a leap year how many days would there be? _____

21. Circle one full week.

22. How many Sundays are in this month? _____

23. What day of the week is the 15th of this month? _____

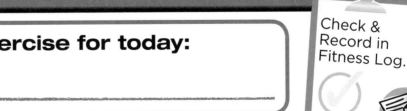

Choose your AEROBIC exercise!

Exercise for today:

Check & Record in Fitness Log.

Day 8

An Attitude of Gratitude

Gratitude is the feeling of being thankful. It is when you thank someone for the good things they have done for you or given to you. Scientists have found that having a grateful attitude can help you have a happier, healthier life.

How many smaller words can you make from the letters in "GRATITUDE"?

_____   _____   _____

_____   _____   _____

_____   _____   _____

_____   _____   _____

Think of things you are grateful for. Make a list of at least 10 things:

1. _____

2. _____

3. _____

4. _____

5. _____

6. _____

7. _____

8. _____

9. _____

10. _____

There are many ways to say thank you. Unscramble these words to say thank you in another language. The beginning letter has been given to you.

French	Spanish	German
11. <u>ercim</u> = m _____	12. <u>ragacsi</u> = g _____	13. <u>kande</u> = d _____

- Each day write down or share at least three good things about your day.
- Remember to say thank you throughout the day.
- Write thank you cards immediately after receiving a gift.
- Tell your parents, family, and friends how much you appreciate them.

Add or subtract. Simplify.

1. 2/7 + 4/7 = _____

2. 6/9 – 3/9 = _____

3. 1/4 + 1/4 = _____

4. 4/15 + 6/15 = _____

5. 11/12 – 5/12 = _____

6. 3/10 + 4/10 = _____

7. 11/19 – 7/19 = _____

8. 12/20 + 4/20 = _____

9. 9/11- 7/11 = _____

Simplify each fraction. Ex. 2/4 = 1/2

10. 3/9 = _____

11. 2/6 = _____

12. 3/6 = _____

13. 4/8 = _____

14. 2/10 = _____

15. 5/15 = _____

The factors of 12 are 1,2,3,4,6, and 12:   (1 x 12 = 12   2 x 6 =12   3 x 4 =12)

What are the factors for each number?

16.   10: _____

17.   18: _____

18.   20: _____

19.   36: _____

Solve for x   Ex. 3 x = 9   x = 3

20. 5 x = 25   x = _____

21. 4 x = 16   x = _____

22. 10 x = 100   x = _____

23. 6 x = 24   x = _____

24. 12 x = 120   x = _____

25. 2 x = 50   x = _____

Choose your STRENGTH exercise!

Exercise for today:

_____

Day 9

Check & Record in Fitness Log.

FRIENDSHIP

Value

Friendship is spending time with someone else that you care about — animals or people!

KARTICK

Kartick grew up in India near Bannerghatta National Park where he learned to love animals and nature. At night he would go into the park and watch different animals including sloth bears, elephants and leopards drink water from fresh pools under the moonlight. He showed them respect and did not scare them off by being loud or disruptive. He grew to love the animals very much and cared for their safety. He grew to see the animals as his friends and knew that he needed to protect them. The first animals that Kartick protected were the sloth bears that were also known as "Dancing Bears" because people trained them to dance for entertainment and did not treat them well. Kartick and his organization Wildlife SOS freed all the bears by teaching their owners to do different jobs for money like operate taxis and gas stations and to let their bears go. In 2015 Kartick and Wildlife SOS freed Raju the elephant from years of captivity. Raju was also being used to entertain on the streets. She was treated very badly to make sure that she obeyed. When Raju was freed she was so happy that a big elephant tear rolled down her cheek! Raju now lives with other elephants that have been freed.

1. **Write a short story about an adventure — fiction or fact — with your best friend. Your friend can be an animal or person! Use a separate piece of paper to continue your story and add drawing!**

_____

_____

_____

2. **Put these words in alphabetical order:**

India _____

bear _____

wildlife _____

happy _____

friends _____

Value: FRIENDSHIP

"Don't walk behind me; I may not lead. Don't walk in front of me; I may not follow. Just walk beside me and be my friend."

– Winnie the Pooh

```
H O N E S T W S Q M M H B E T O H L
P K K P K H U C V C Z S E R U D R U
G D X D O O C P P B H N U F E M S F
W A K W R Y R F I A G D V A Z D Q T
F U V E L O P D N J I V C A O S Y C
E G N M K L Y U O K L P E K W J R E
Y E L K K L I E H H O Q H H O O T P
G I J I K T D S U T Y Z Z C T M W S
E K N B A P Y K T J A M R D O Z B E
N D C U W T P X U E L L P W B G K R
Z R Y B W L M B K S N N R Q Z D B H
X R G G U F Q J S R P P S T K I M V
G W V C U K B D R Z W N N V G T A B
U P G J G K L D G X U T H B R I C I
Y I A F Q S X S U I B P R L L H E P
K N I P F B J Y D M R K U O J T Q P
```

Find the words below that are qualities of a good friend.

WORD BANK

fun	listen
loyal	generous
honest	respectful
kind	

Be a Good Friend

 Invite a friend over. Let them choose what to play first.

 Watch *Toy Story* with your family. Talk about how the characters in the movie portray true friendship.

 Make a friendship bracelet for one of your friends. Give it to them and tell them why you are happy to be friends.

 **Day 10**

Choose a **Play** or **Exercise** Activity!

3-4 • © Summer Fit Activities™

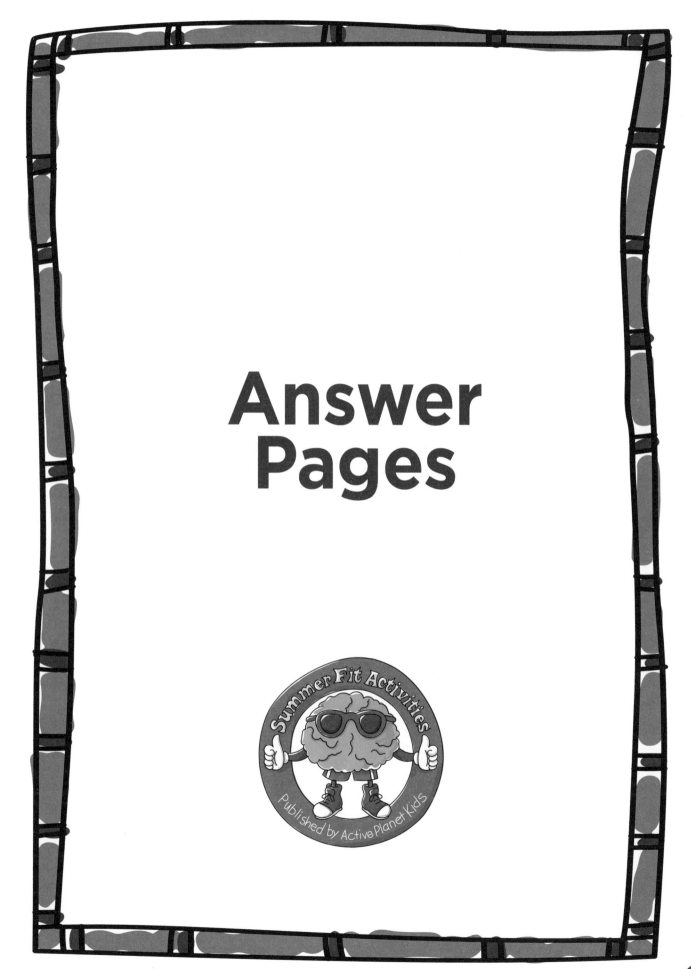

Answer Pages

3-4 • © Summer Fit Activities™

Answer Key

P. 1-4
Summer Skills Review
1. 5,215
2. a. 4,436   b. 9,812
3. 2,000
4. 114,134,364,411.
5. 2,8,7,6.
6. a. 150   b. 80   c. 650
7. a. 600   b. 100   c. 800
8. 3,000 + 900 + 70 + 4
9. a. 549   b. 7,822   c. 2,559   d. 406
10. 14,5,8,21,12,9,18,35,32,24,18, 56
   ,45,56,48,22,54,36,27,16,36,15,
   64,42,12.
11. a. 1,304   b. 9,380
   c. 61,074   d. 16,328
12. a. 5   b. 4   c. 6   d. 6
   e. 6   f. 9   g. 10   h. 6
13. a. 15 r. 2   b. 61   c. 961   d. 347
14. a. 1/2 colored   b. 1/4 colored
   c. 1/3 colored   d. 2/4 colored.
15. small, gray, tile, tiny.
16. a. Ouch! That hurt!
   b. What time does the movie start?
   c. I am so happy to be on summer vacation.
17. a. afraid   b. smart   c. complete
   (answers may vary.
18. a. below   b. light   c. hot
   (answers may vary.
19. Aunt Megan, Seattle, Washington.
20. John, Joseph,
21. factory, freedom, giant, group, harbor.
22. a. pair   b. read
23. a. I'll   b. you're   c. it's
24. a. wolves   b. babies   c. girls
25. a. er   b. est   c. ing
26. c   27. as-tro-naut
28. noon, spoon, raccoon, balloon
   (answers vary.
29. a. am   b. does   c. an   d. there

p. 7:
1. not very often   2. feeling bad
3. enjoys it   4. teasing me
5. understand   6. taking a risk
7. pouring rain   8. wiggling around
9. go to bed   10. day dreaming
11. go ahead and eat
12. don't know what to say   13. easy

p. 8:
1. 60   2. 170   3. 290
4. 360   5. 100   6. 390
7. 130   8. 800   9. 100
10. 200   11. 600   12. 4,000
13. 5,200   14. 8,400   15. 2,000
16. 8,000   17. 5,000   18. 1,000
19. 2,000   20. 5,000   21. 7,000
22. 10,000   23. 8,000

p. 9:
1. arachnid
2. eight legs, two
body parts, many eyes
3. vibrations they feel with tiny hairs
4. molt   5. spinnerets
6. head, abdomen

p. 10:
Prime Numbers (2,3,5,7,11,13,17,19,23,
   29,31,37,41,43,47)
Square around number one; 8, 24,
   12, 16, 45

p. 11:
1. dry   2. asleep   3. sad
4. go   5. float   6. white
7. loud   8. couch   9. huge
10. smart   11. fair   12. happy
13. yelled

p. 12:
1. 1   2. 3   3. 2   4. 2
5. 3   6. 1   7. 2   8. 1
9. 3   10. 22   11. 5   12. 4

● Right
● Obtuse
● Acute

p. 13: Answers Vary
1. beautiful, strong, honest
2. rotten, smelly
3. creative, studios, trustworthy
4. hot, lazy, busy
5. funny, kind, honest
6. sweet, juicy, delicious
7. delicious, chocolate, 8th
8. soft, furry, tiny
9. striped, new, blue

p. 14:
Row 1: (3) 3, 12, 18, 9, 15, 27, 24, 21, 6, 30
Row 2: (6) 6, 24, 36, 18, 30, 54, 48, 42, 12, 60
Row 3: (9) 9, 36, 54, 27, 45, 81, 72, 63, 18, 90
Row 4: (4) 4, 16, 24, 12, 20, 36, 32, 28, 8, 40
Row 5: (1) 1, 4, 6, 3, 5, 9, 8, 7, 2, 10
Row 6: (5) 5, 20, 30, 15, 25, 45, 40, 35, 10, 50
Row 7: (7) 7, 28, 42, 21, 35, 63, 56, 49, 14, 70
Row 8: (2) 2, 8, 12, 6, 10, 18, 16, 14, 4, 20
Row 9: (10) 10, 40, 60, 30, 50, 90, 80, 70, 20, 100
Row 10: (8) 8, 32, 48, 24, 40, 72, 64, 56, 16, 80
11. 138   12. 42

p. 15:
1. log cabin   2. read   3. honesty
4. president   5. slavery

p. 19:
1. geese   2. mice   3. boxes
4. boys   5. dogs   6. babies
7. men   8. puppies   9. tables
10. calves   11. coats   12. fish
13. watches   14. wolves   15. leaves
16. ladies   17. bunnies 18. monkeys
19. dishes   20. letters

p. 20:
1. yes   2. no   3. no
4. no   5. yes   6. no

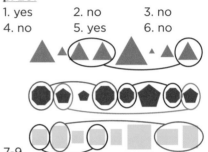

7-9.

p. 21:
1. will   2. am   3. were   4. are
5. is   6. was   7. my, her   8. her, hers
9. our   10. your   11. their   12. my, her
13. our, its   14. his, his   15. her, hers
16. mine, yours

Correct work
every day or
two to help
keep students
accountable.
This also shows
your child you
are interested in
their work.

Answer Key

p. 22:
1. VI 2. VIII 3. II 4. IV
5. X 6. V 7. XIII 8. IX
9. 20, 17, 19, 27, 100, 4, 62, 40, 23
10. XXXVI, LV, XIV, XXIX, XL, XXI
11. II, IV, V, VII, VIII, IX, XI, XII

p. 23:
1. Prefix = re; Root Word = wash; wash again
2. Prefix = ex;
    Root Word = change; change from
3. Prefix = re; Root Word = build; build again
4. Prefix = de; Root Word = crease; make less
5. Prefix = re; RootWord = teach; teach again
6. Prefix = de; Root Word = tour; tour away
7. Prefix = pre;
    Root Word = school; before kindergarten
8. Prefix = re; Root Word = do; do again
9. Prefix = pre; Root Word = pay; pay before
10. Prefix = ex; Root Word = claim; speak out
11-13. Answers Vary

p. 24:
1. 925 2. 7,416 3. 375
4. 214 5. Three hundred twenty
6. One thousand eight hundred fiftytwo
7. Five thousand two hundred forty-eight
8. Three thousand nine hundred eighty
9. 500 + 90 + 8
10. 4,000 + 300 + 60 +7
11. 6,000 + 700 + 80 + 1
12. 8,000 + 100 + 3
13. 1,743 14. 3,529 15. 9,265
16. 5,982 17. 300 18. 600
19. 65 20. 7,000 21. 85 22. 200

p. 25:
1. hummingbird 2. woodpecker
3. chameleon 4. penguin
5. capybara 6. raccoon
Extra credit: South America;
    North America; hum-ming-bird;
    wood-peck-er; cap-y-bar-a

p. 26:
1. 3/8; 2. 2/3; 3. 1/2;
4. 3/10; 5. 5/9; 6. 5/6;
7. = 8. < 9-11 Answers Shaded

p. 27: 1-6 Answers Vary

p. 31:
1. a child's imagination
2. dark brown
3. leaves, castles, boats
4. far away 5. more/ashore
6. answers vary

p. 32:
1. 12,15,30,27,6,18,24,3,21,9
2. 36,12,30,24,54,18,42,60,48,6
3. 20,12,4,40,24,8,28,16,36,32
4. 24,80,48,64,16,32,8,56,72,40
5. 50,5,30,10,20,40,35,15,45,25
6. 21,14,56,63,35,49,28,42,7,70

p. 33:
1. thing 2. thing 3. place
4. person 5. thing 6. place
7. person 8. person 9. place
10. thing 11. place 12. person
13. person 14. thing 15. place
16. movie 17. month 18. state
19. holiday 20. store 21. street
22. dog 23. boy 24–31. answers vary

p. 34:
1. 143 2. 698 3. 549
4. 534 5. 251 6. 552
7. 211 8. 289 9. 2
10. 40 11. 7 12. 48
13. 5 14. 10 15. 4
16. 36 17. 3 18. 4 19. 16
20. 40,35,30,25,20,15,10,5
21. 26,28,30,32,34,36,38,40
22. 18,21,24,27,30,33,36,39
23. 150,160,170,180,190,200,210,220

p. 35:
1. verbs; run, whisper, swim, hop,
    sing, crawl, eat, jump, drink, bark
2. swim, swam, will swim
3. play, played, will play
4. sing, sang, will sing
5. draw, drew, will draw

p. 36:
1. 120 2. 97 3. 148 4. 80
5. 24 6. 20 7. 12 8. 20 9. 22
10. 19 11. 50 12. 100 13. 299,301
14. 18 15. 349 16. 1277
17. 4,999, 5,001 18. 9,000 19. 1,000
20. 6:45 21. 2:25 22. 10:05

p. 37:
1. tail 2. week 3. too
4. read 5. know 6. write
7. where 8. flour 9. due
10. peak 11. male 12. leak

p. 38:
1. 16cm 2. 20cm 3. 22cm
4. 36cm 5. 34cm 6. 15cm
7. 6cm 8. 44cm 9. 52cm
10. each side is 2cm

p. 39:
1. she did what she said
2. helped others while risking her life
3. kept her word 4. helped the slaves
5-6. answers vary

p. 43:
1. out 2. water 3. woman
4. school 5. sad 6. vegetable
7. night 8. leg 9. hear
10. cold 11. book 12. sheep

p. 44:
1. $1.96 2. $1.60 3. $1.89
4. $8.10 5. $ .35 6. $5.95
7. answers vary
8. $1.25, $6.70, $10.50, $15.00,
    $59.75, $25.50, $.09, $12.46,
    $100.65

p. 45:
1. payment 2. washable
3. frighten 4. breakable
5. invention 6. improvement
7. soften 8. direction
9. collected 10. careful 11. fearless
12. louder 13. fastest 14. walking
15. gladness 16. neater
17. thoughtless 18. cheated
19. sleeping 20. safely

Reward well done and completed work with stickers, stamps or hand written messages.

3-4 • © Summer Fit Activities™

Answer Key

p. 45: cont
21. root=happy;pre=un;suffix=ness
22. root=pack;pre=un;suffix=ing
23. root=frost;pre=de;suffix=ed
24. root=paint;pre=re;suffix=ed
25. root=correct;pre=in;suffix=ly
26. root=claim;pre=ex;suffix=ed
27. root=perfect;pre=im;suffix=ly
28. root=comfort;pre=un;suffix=able

p. 46:
1. 1,560   2. 5,650   3. 5,650
4. 506   5. 56   6. 600   7. 60
8. 6,000   9. 6   10. 50   11. 500
12. 5   13. 5,000   14. 20
15. 200   16. 2   17. 2,000
18. 89,129,568,652,1,067

p. 47:
1. 200   2. calcium
3. brain, heart, lungs
4. bone marrow   5. blood cells
6. femur   7. 12

p. 48:
1. 8:16   2. 8:50   3. 11:25
4. 3:10   5. 6:40   6. 12:25   7. 9:35
8. 12:15   9. eighteen minutes after three
10. five minutes before three
11. twenty nine minutes after seven
12. twenty five minutes before ten

Use a timer to motivate your child to stay on task and finish their work in a timely manner.

p. 49:
1. hard   2. dark   3. whisper
4. walk   5. laugh   6. careful
7. clean   8. happy   9. near
10. low   11. over   12. hot
13. in   14. down   15. stop
16. awake   17. lose

p. 50:
1. 8,001   2. 6,462   3. 12,247
4. 2,252   5. 2,402   6. 4,420
7. 3,522   8. 2,192   9. 77
10. 140   11. 99   12. 175
13. 530   14. 109   15. 258
16. 617   17. 667   18. 209
19. 589   20. 1,034   21. 178
22. 433   23. 9,790   24. 1,664

p. 51:
1. F   2. T   3. F   4. T   5. T . F

p. 55:
1. Joseph had a sleepover with his friends Brendan, Jacob, and Sam.
2. I am going to visit my friend Isabella in San Diego, California.
3. Ouch! A mosquito bit me on the leg!
4. "Christmas is my favorite holiday," said Beth.
5. Mom packed us a delicious picnic lunch of sandwiches, chips, carrot sticks, and cookies.
6. Grandma's favorite hobby is water skiing on Bear Lake.
7. Jonathan and Noah went to the circus on Saturday.
8. Amy watered the plants and pulled the weeds in the garden.
9. Ants use their antennae to smell, touch, and find food.

p. 56:
Draw 25 triangles, five in each row and divide 25 by 5.
1. 8   2. 6   3. 4   4. 3   5. 7
6. 9   7. 4   8. 5   9. 4   10. 5 r2
11. 61   12. 9 r6   13. 32   14. 23 r3
15. 159   16. 218   17. 844

p. 57:
1. Idaho   2. Olympia   3. Utah
4. Arizona   5. Canada   6. California
7. Pacific Ocean   8. Salem
9. California, Nevada, Utah, Colorado, New Mexico
10. New Mexico

p. 58: Heart

p. 59:
1. 2,2,2   2. 5,5,5   3. 1,1,1,
4. 4,3,3   5. 4,4,4   6. 2,2,2
7. 3,3,3   8. 2,2,2   9. 4,4,4
(circle dictionary)   10. ba-na-na
11. be-cause   12. flow-ers
13. neigh-bor-ly   14. wood-peck-er
15. sweat-er   16. book-case
17. re-al-ize   18. hap-pi-ness

p. 60:
1. 4,914   2. 1,377   3. 6,311
4. 42,068   5. 100,845   6. 2,592
7. 344,760   8. 735   9. 12
10. 24   11. 7   12. 3
13. 2   14. 1   15. 60
16. 36   17. 2

p. 61:
1. sun   2. precipitation
3. condensation   4. water

p. 62:
1. equilateral   2. isosceles
3. right   4. isosceles   5. right
6. scalene   7. equilateral   8. right

p. 63:
1. Scored 2 goals for Brazil in World Championship game, he entertained fans, no one could stop him from scoring
2. Humanitarian: A person who promotes health and happiness for people
Extraordinary: Unusual, special, remarkable

p. 67:
1. 3 kinds of rocks   2. chapter 5
3. chapter 6   4. p. 20
5. p. 12   6. chapter 4
7. he'll   8. can't   9. you're
10. I'm   11. they've   12. she's
13. hasn't   14. we'll   15. we're
16. isn't   17. they're   18. won't

p. 68:
1. 0.8   2. .7   3. .75
4. .9   5. .5   6. .3
7. .10   8. .90   9. 1/4
10. 6/10   11. 2/10   12. 5/10
13. 4/10   14. 75/100   15. 4/10
16. 9/10   17. 15/100   18. 35/100
19. 1/5   20. 1/2   21. 2/3
22. 4/5   23. 1/10   24. 4/7

Answer Key

p. 69:
1. T   2. T
3. F; Bats like to live in colonies
4. T   5. F; Bats are not birds.   6.T
7. F; Bats use sonar called echolocation
8. F; Most bats eat insects   9. T

p. 70:
1. 6   2. 8   3. 9
4. 3   5. 12   6. 10
7. 9   8. 4
9. 86,680,806,860
10. 154,456,540,654
11. 70,78,87,107
12. 105,450,505,555
13. 59,56,53,50,47
14. 28,35,42,49,56
15. 74,72,70,68,66
16. 130,135,140,145,150
17. 170,160,150,140,130
18. 62,64,66,68,70
19. 132, 3,370, 350, 124
20. 676, 5,334, 445, 1,707
21. 689, 98, 460, 251
22. 2,460, 1,793, 2,890, 230

p. 71:
1. patiently;adverb
2. loudly;adverb
3. brightly;adverb
4. tirelessly;adverb
5. curly;adjective
6. smelly;adjective
7. bravely;adverb
8. gently;adverb
9. friendly;adjective
10. quickly;adverb
11. beautiful;ballerina
12. shy;boy
13. pretty;bouquet
14. fluffy;kitten
15. marching;band
16. patient; librarian, large:group
17-20. Answers Vary

p. 72:
1. > 2. < 3. < 4. < 5. <
6. > 7. < 8. = 9. < 10. <
11. < 12. = 13. > 14. = 15. >
16. = 17. feet 18. feet 19. yards
20. miles 21. inches 22. centimeters
23. quart 24. inch   25. mile
26. week   27. minute   28. pound
29. yard   30. dime

p 73:
1. big spider; built a web under the porch
2. Amanda and Rachel; visited the Doll and Toy Museum
3. space alien; landed his ship in the field
4. Joe and his brother; played in the chest tournament
5. children; played in the sandbox
6. moon and stars; shone brightly in the sky
7. horse; galloped across the field
8. We; rode the bus to the zoo
9-10. Answers Vary

p 74:
1. 100 F   2. 10 C   3. 40 F
4. 212   5. 0   6. thermometer
7. color in thermometer

p 75: Answers Vary
p. 79: Answers Vary

p. 80:
1. $1.00   2. $2.00   3. $2.00
4. $20.00   5. $13.00   6. $6.00
7. $9.00   8. $13.00   9. $16.00
10. $8.00   11. $.88   12. $2.15
13. $41.50   14. $48.75   15. $38.58
16. $102.14 17. $167.00 18. $122.70

p. 81:
1. house   2. button 3. cats & dogs
4. rock   5. baby   6. pancake
7. glove   8. hyena
9. old shoe   10-12. Answers Vary

p.82:
1. 4   2. 5   3. 6   4. 5   5. 6
6. $.50 7. $.25 8. 8 9. 8
10. 20 11. 41 12. 13   13. 14

p. 83:
1-8. Check your work with a map of the United States of America

p. 84:
1. 0-9-8-7   2. 1-2-7-6
3. 5-8-2-0   4. 0-6-9-4
5. 9-0-4-1   6. 8-3-4-9
(7-10) 6 + 6 + 6 ;
     3+3+3+3+3+3;
     6 x 3; 3 x 6
(11-14) 8 + 8 + 8 + 8 ;
     4 + 4 + 4 + 4 + 4 + 4 + 4 + 4;
     4 x 8; 8 x 4
15. 8:15   16. 7:50

p. 85:
1. is   2. are   3. were
4. was   5. am   6. am
7. are   8. were   9. are   10. is

p. 86:
1. parallel   2. perpendicular
3. intersecting   4. intersecting
5. parallel   6. intersecting
7. one   8. two   9. one
10. two   11. one   12. two

p. 87:
1. worthless 2. weakness
3. lose   4. arrogant
5. war   6. help
7. Answers Vary

p. 91:
1. 90%
2. Arctic, Southern, Indian, Atlantic, Pacific
3. Explores and studies the ocean and all that it contains.
   A vessel capable of operating or remaining under water

p. 92:
1. March   2. April
3. 60   4. 90
5. 10,15,25,50,60,65,90,95,100
6. 90

Have your child correct their own work while you read off the answers. This will reinforce the skills they just practiced.

Answer Key

p. 93:
1. mowed   2. ate   3. toasted
4. chirped   5. boils   6. playing
7. cooking   8. making   9. will skate
10. will catch   11. will hatch
12. will practice

p. 94:
1. 8:45; 10:30; 15 minutes
2. 3:35; 2:45; 40 minutes
3. 11:35; 12:55; 40 minutes
4. $48.00   5. $3.13   6. 8 cookies

p. 95:
firm, fish, fishhook, first, fisherman
1. 4,3,5,2,1   2. 1,2,3,4,5
3. 5,4,3,1,2   4. 1,4,2,5,3

p. 96:
1. $3.10   2. $1.90   3. $6.50
4. $3.50   5. no, $.35   6. salad
7. fries   8. $7.20

p. 97: Answers Vary

p. 98:
1. 12   2. 35   3. 72
4. 48   5. 50   6. 32

p. 99:
1. Canada   2. cancer
3. research   4. money
5. Hope
6. amputate; Cut off (a limb.,
   typically by surgical operation)

Give your student an opportunity to rework missed questions. Go over any mistakes made together.

p. 103:
Faster, fastest, swimmer, swimming,
   longer, longest, etc.
Continue making as many new
   words as you can.

p. 104:
1. 2 1/3   2. 7/4 = 1 3/4
3. 5/7   4. 4/5   5. 3/4
6. 1/4   7. 7/7 = 1   8. 6/5 = 1 1/5
9. 9/9 = 1   10. <   11. >
12. >   13. >   14. =
15. =   16. <   17. <
18. <   19. 3/9, 4/9, 5/9, 7/9

p. 105:
1. S
2. F; Birds build nests in trees.
3. S
4. F; The dog didn't like being left in
   the rain.
5. S
6. F; I liked to ride my bike.
7. F; My uncle is a shoe salesman.
8. S
9. F; I wish I could go to the moon.
10. S
11. F; The camping trip was fun.
12. S   13. a   14. an
15. a   16. an   17. an
18. a   19. an   20. a
21. an   22. a   23. an

p. 106:
Use calculator to check your
   answers.

p. 107:
1. swamp   2. desert
3. ocean   4. forest

p. 108:
1. 2,677   2. 458   3. 19,461
4. 21,600   5. 9,072   6. 8,073
7. 30,40,50 8. 170, 180, 190
9. 360, 370, 380
10. 780, 770, 760
11. 1,230, 1,240, 1250
12. 5,650, 5,640, 5,630
13. 32   14. 36   15. 6
16. 9   17. 8   18. 80
19. 27   20. 56   21. 7
22. 4   23. 36   24. 21

p. 109: Answers Vary

p. 110:
1. three   2. two   3. two
4. two   5. zero (asymmetrical)
6. none   7. two   8. none
9. four   10-12. draw the other half

p. 111: Answers Vary
p. 115: Answers Vary

p. 116:
1. dozen   2. feet   3. pounds
4. gallon   5. ounces   6. yards
7. years   8. dollars   9. miles
10. inches   11. hour   12. minutes

p. 117:
1. chalk   2. once
3. photograph   4. weigh
5. column   6. entertain
7. solemn   8. handle
9. knowledge   10. neighbor

p. 118:
1. 8   2. 2   3. apples
4. 4   5. pineapple   6. 32

p. 119:
1. peninsula 2. plain 3. volcano 4. valley
5. mountain 6. island 7. plateau

p. 120:
1. Jan.   2. Oct.   3. Aug.
4. June   5. Apr.   6. Feb.
7. Nov.   8. Sept.   9. July
10. May   11. Mar.   12. Dec.
13. 12   14. 7   15. 365, 366
16. weeks   17. February   18. 4
19. No   20. 29   21. Answers shows
one week circled 22. 4 23. Tuesday

p. 121:
1-10. Answers Vary
11. Merci   12. Gracias   13. Danke
p. 122:
1. 6/7   2. 1/3   3. 1/2   4. 2/3
5. 1/2   6. 7/10   7. 4/19   8. 4/5
9. 2/11   10. 1/3   11. 1/3   12. 1/2
13. 1/2   14. 1/5   15. 1/3
16. 1,2,5,10   17. 1,2,3,6,9,18
18. 1, 2,4,5,10,20   19. 1,3,4,6,9,12,18,36
20. 5   21. 4   22. 10
23. 4   24. 10   25. 25

p. 123:
1. Story will vary. Read for
    creativity, grammar and overall
    comprehension
2. Bear, friends, happy, India,
    wildlife

Summer Fit Book Report I

Title: _____

Author: _____

Illustrator: _____

Setting (Where the story takes place): _____

Main Character(s):

_____

_____

_____

Write your favorite part of the story
(use separate sheet of paper if needed):

_____

_____

_____

_____

_____

_____

_____

_____

_____

_____

Tell your favorite part of the story to a parent, guardian or friend.

Read a variety of books on topics that interest you already and new areas that you want to explore!

3-4 • © Summer Fit Activities™

Summer Fit Book Report II

Title: _____

Author: _____

Illustrator: _____

Setting (Where the story takes place): _____

Main Character(s):

_____

_____

_____

Write your favorite part of the story
(use separate sheet of paper if needed):

_____

_____

_____

_____

_____

_____

_____

_____

_____

Tell your favorite part of the story to a parent, guardian or friend.

Read a variety of books on topics that interest you already and new areas that you want to explore!

Summer Fit Book Report III

Title: _____

Author: _____

Illustrator: _____

Setting (Where the story takes place): _____

Main Character(s):

_____

_____

_____

Write your favorite part of the story
(use separate sheet of paper if needed):

_____

_____

_____

_____

_____

_____

_____

_____

_____

Tell your favorite part of the story to a parent, guardian or friend.

Read a variety of books on topics that interest you already and new areas that you want to explore!

133

Summer Fit Book Report IV

Title: _____

Author: _____

Illustrator: _____

Setting (Where the story takes place): _____

Main Character(s):

_____

_____

_____

Write your favorite part of the story
(use separate sheet of paper if needed):

_____

_____

_____

_____

_____

_____

_____

_____

_____

_____

Tell your favorite part of the story to a parent, guardian or friend.

Read a variety of books on topics that interest you already and new areas that you want to explore!

HEALTH
&
NUTRITION

Summer Fit Activities
Published by Active Planet Kids

Let's Play

There are so many ways to play! Check off the different activities as you play them, have fun!

Everybody has different abilities and interests, so take the time to figure out what activities and exercises you like. Try them all: soccer, dance, karate, basketball and skating are only a few. After you have played a lot of different ones, go back and focus on the ones you like! Create your own ways to be active and combine different activities and sports to put your own twist on things. Talk with your parents or caregiver for ideas and have them help you find and do the activities that you like best. Playing and exercising is a great way to help you become fit, but remember that the most important thing about playing is that you are having fun!

List of Exercise Activities

Home–Outdoor:

Walking
Ride Bicycle
Swimming
Walk Dog
Golf with whiffle balls outside
Neighborhood walks/Exploring (in a safe area)
Hula Hooping
Rollerskating/Rollerblading
Skateboarding
Jump rope
Climbing trees
Play in the back yard
Hopscotch
Stretching
Basketball
Yard work
Housecleaning

Home – Indoor:

Dancing
Exercise DVD
Yoga DVD
Home gym equipment
Stretch bands
Free weights
Stretching

With friends or family:

Red Rover
Chinese jump rope
Regular jump rope
Ring around the rosie
Tag/Freeze
Four score
Capture the flag
Dodgeball
Slip n Slide
Wallball
Tug of War
Stretching
Run through a sprinkler
Skipping
Family swim time
Bowling
Basketball
Hiking
Red light, Green light
Kick ball
Four Square
Tennis
Frisbee
Soccer
Jump Rope
Baseball

Turn off TV Go Outside – PLAY!
Public Service Announcement
Brought to you by Summer Fit

Chill out on Screen Time

Screen time is the amount of time spent watching TV, DVDs or going to the movies, playing video games, texting on the phone and using the computer. The more time you spend looking at a screen the less time you are outside riding your bike, walking, swimming or playing soccer with your friends. Try to spend no more than a couple hours a day in front of a screen for activities other than homework and get outside and play!

HEALTHY BODIES

There are many ways to enrich your life by eating healthy, exercising each day and playing! Keeping your body strong and healthy will help you feel good and even perform better in school. To be healthy, you need to eat right, get enough sleep and exercise. What you learn and do with Summer Fit Activities™ is just the beginning. From here, you will be able to find other healthy and active things to do based on your interests, abilities and personal goals.

 Aerobic Exercises help your cardiovascular system that includes your heart and blood vessels. You need a strong heart to pump blood. Your blood delivers oxygen and nutrients to your body.

 Strength Exercises help you make your muscles stronger and increase your muscular endurance. Endurance helps you get the most from your muscles before you get tired!!

 Flexibility Exercises are good for many reasons including warming up before you do aerobic or strength exercises. Flexibility also helps you use all your muscles in different ways, positions and ranges of motion.

Your body composition is made up of lean mass and fat mass. Lean mass includes water, muscles and organs in your body. Fat mass includes fat your body needs for later and stores for energy.

Exercise helps you burn body fat and do more of the activities you want to do like hiking, biking and playing at the beach. There are a lot fun sports and activities to choose from that will help you strengthen your body and your brain!

Get Active!

Apple	Brain
Water	Vegetable
Exercise	Muscles
Aerobic	Organs
Strength	Fun
Flexibility	Play

```
D G L H B J S Z V Z B R F P C
Y H V T T E V E V A Z Y L F I
A C U P L G G M Y K I V E S B
G O T C A E N G H T P W X M O
H E S X T L M E Y A L P I L R
A U Y A E S I C R E X E B V E
M P B Y B M R G B T H Z I Q A
I L P R O L S V V F S R L K X
E Y A L D P E N B G A R I I I
F I B P E L H Y U V I F T W N
N G T D J A U D L F Z Q Y A X
O N M C X A V R S I V J S T J
O R G A N S B W A K K R A E C
J T C E L Y R C U Z R B G R P
X J P Y A W W E O S C K I K J
```

3-4 • © Summer Fit Activities™

Active Lifestyle Pop Quiz!

What does being active mean to you?

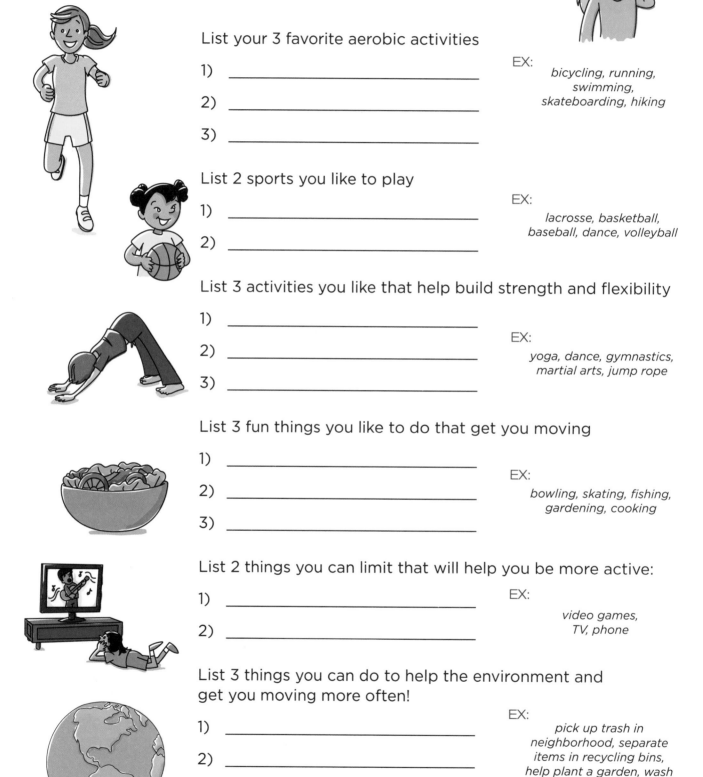

List your 3 favorite aerobic activities

1) _____

2) _____

3) _____

EX:

bicycling, running, swimming, skateboarding, hiking

List 2 sports you like to play

1) _____

2) _____

EX:

lacrosse, basketball, baseball, dance, volleyball

List 3 activities you like that help build strength and flexibility

1) _____

2) _____

3) _____

EX:

yoga, dance, gymnastics, martial arts, jump rope

List 3 fun things you like to do that get you moving

1) _____

2) _____

3) _____

EX:

bowling, skating, fishing, gardening, cooking

List 2 things you can limit that will help you be more active:

1) _____

2) _____

EX:

video games, TV, phone

List 3 things you can do to help the environment and get you moving more often!

1) _____

2) _____

3) _____

EX:

pick up trash in neighborhood, separate items in recycling bins, help plant a garden, wash your water cup and reuse, ride your bike

Summer Fitness Program

The goal of your Summer Fitness program is to help you improve in all areas of physical fitness and to be active every day.

 You build cardiovascular endurance through aerobic exercise. For aerobic exercise, you need to work large muscle groups that get your heart pumping and oxygen moving through your entire body. This increases your heart rate and breathing. On your aerobic day, you can jog, swim, hike, dance, skateboard, ride your bike, roller blade... there are so many to choose from

Your goal should be to try to get 30 minutes a day of aerobic exercise at least 2-3 times a week. Follow your daily Summer Fit™ exercise schedule and choose your own aerobic exercises along the way.

 You build your muscular strength and muscle endurance with exercises that work your muscles, like push-ups, sit-ups and pull-ups. Increase how many you can do of each of these over time and pay attention to your Summer Fit ™daily exercises for other activities that help build strong muscles.

Get loose – stretch. Warming up before you exercise if very important. It prepares your body for exercising by loosening your muscles and getting your body ready for training. An easy start is to shake your arms and roll your shoulders!

Time to Hydrate

It is important to drink water before and after you exercise because water regulates your body temperature and gives you nutrients to keep you healthy.

The next time you exercise, drink a cup of water before and after you are done.

Color the bottom half of the cup red below to represent the water you drink before you exercise. Color the top half of the cup blue to represent the water you drink after you exercise.

Water Facts

There is the same amount of water on earth today as there was when dinosaurs roamed through our backyards!

75% of your brain is water!

Water regulates the earth's temperature.

Water is made up of two elements, hydrogen and oxygen. Its chemical formula is H_2O

Water is essential for life on earth.

Here are instructions for your daily exercises. Talk with a parent about setting goals. Set your goals for time or reps. Keep track of your goals using your Summer Fitness Chart. Have fun!

Aerobic Exercises and Activities

Jogging in Place: Run slowly in place or outside to accomplish your time goal.

Bump and Jump: Jump forward and back, jump side to side. Hop on one foot to another, moving side-to-side, alternating feet. Quicken your pace.

Let's Dance: Step to your right with your right foot (putting your weight on your right foot). Step behind your right foot with your left foot (putting your weight on your left foot). Step again to the right with your right foot (weight on right) and touch your left foot next to your right (with your weight staying on the right foot). Repeat the above going left but switching to the other foot.
Goal = Dance for 5 minutes
Do the Cha-cha Step forward right, cha-cha Step forward left, cha-cha Repeat
Do the Cross over Cross right over left, kick out right leg then backwards cha-cha-cha Cross left over right, kick out left leg then backwards cha-cha-cha Repeat
Do the Rope Rope 1/4 to the left 1/4 facing the rear 1/4 turn left again Rope to the front and step together with a clap. Repeat (When you "rope" hold one hand above your head and swing your arms in a circle like you have a rope above you).

Pass and Go: This activity requires a second person. Ask a friend or someone from your family to play with you. The object of this activity is to pass a ball back and forth counting by 2's get to a 100 as fast as you can. Have a stopwatch handy. Set a time you want to beat and go! Increase your goal by setting a lower time. Repeat.

Step It Up: This activity uses stairs if you have them. If you do, take three trips up and down the stairs. Raise your legs high like you are in a marching band. If you do not have stairs, do 20 step-ups on one step. Start slow and increase your speed.

Kangaroo Bounce: Tape a shoelace to the floor in a straight line. Stand on one side of the string with both feet together. Jump forward over the string and then backward to land in your original place. Take a short break—and do it again. This time jump side-to-side over the shoelace.

Garbage Hoops: A trashcan makes a great indoor basketball goal— perfect for a quick game of one-on-one against yourself or a friend! Use a bottle-cap or crunched up ball of paper as your basketball. Twist, jump and make sure to use a few fakes to win the game! First one to 11 wins!

Green Giant: Mow the grass, weed the garden or pick up your yard. Feeling good today? Mow your neighbors yard too!

Capture the Flag: Use scarves or old T-shirts for flags. Assign a different color one for each team. Use chalk, cones, tape, or landmarks such as trees or sidewalks to divide your playing area into equal-sized territories for each team. Place one flag into each territory. It must be visible and once it is placed it cannot be moved. When the game begins, players cross into opposing teams' territories to grab their flags. When a player is in an opposing team's territory they can be captured by the other team. Once they are tagged he/she must run to the sideline and perform an exercise—for example, five jumping jacks or three push-ups. After they perform their exercise the player can go back to their team territory and resume play. The game ends when one team successfully captures the flag(s) from the other team or teams and returns to their own territory with the opposing team's flag.

Happy Feet: Use your feet every chance you get today. Walk to a friend's house, to the store, around the park or wherever it's safe to walk. Get your parents to walk with you after dinner.

Let's Roll: Put your lungs to work on your bike, skates or scooter. Don't forget to wear helmets and pads!

Speed: Walk a block, than run as fast as you can the next block. Alternate between walking and running blocks. Rest in between. Time yourself and see if you can beat your original time. Repeat. **Goal = 2 blocks**

Tag: Decide who is "IT." Choose the boundaries for the game. If a player crosses the boundaries during the game, he/she is automatically "IT."
Give players a 15 second head start. "IT" counts to 15 and then chases the others to tag them! The player who has been tagged is now "IT!"

Hide and Seek: Select an area to play. Designate a specific area with clear boundaries. Have everyone gather around a tree or other landmark, which is "home base." Whoever goes first must close his/her eyes and count to 10. Everybody else hides during the count. After the count is over, call out "Ready or not here I come!" Now it's time to look for the other players who are hiding. They are trying to get to home base before they are found. If they get to home base without being found they are "safe." The first player found loses and they start the next game by counting to 10!

Hula-Hoop: Hold the hula-hoop around your waist with both hands. Pull it forward so it is resting against your back. With both hands, fling the hoop to the left so that rolls in a circle around your body. Do this a few times until you get the feel of it. Leave the hula-hoop on the ground for a few minutes and practice swirling your hip. Move your pelvis left, back, right, forward. Find a groove and keep the hoop going around your hips as long as you can. When it falls to the ground pick it up and try again!

Jump Rope: Start by holding an end of the rope in each hand. Position the rope behind you on the ground. Raise your arms up and turn the rope over your head bringing it down in front of you. When it reaches the ground, jump over it. Find a good pace, not too slow and not too fast. Jump over the rope each time it comes around. Continue until you reach your goal of jumping a certain amount of times without stopping.

Strength Exercises and Activities

Knee lifts: Stand with your feet flat on the floor. Start by lifting your right knee up 5 times, always bring both feet together between each interval then change legs. When you feel more confident, bounce while you bring your knee up and alternate between legs.

Pushups: Start in an elevated position. Keep your body straight, head facing forward. Lower yourself down by bending your elbows. Once your chest touches the ground, push back up to your starting position.

Curl-ups: Start by lying on the floor, knees bent and arms crossed in front. Rise up and forward until your chest touches your raised knee. As soon as you touch your knee, go back down slowly to your starting position.

Squats: Stand up straight with your legs shoulder width apart. Keep your ankles and legs pointed straight forward. Raise your arms in front of you during the exercise. Bend your knees and lower yourself down like you are going to sit in a chair until your bottom is in a straight line with your knees while keeping your back straight. If you cannot make it down this far, go as far as you can, hold for two seconds and slowly raise back up to your starting position.

Chop n Squat: Start with legs wide, bring your feet together, then out wide again, reach down and touch the ground, and pop up.

Chin Ups: Start by hanging from the bar with your arms fully extended, keeping your feet off the ground. Your hands should be facing into the bar with your palms on the bar itself. Pull yourself up until your chin touches the bar. When you touch the bar with your chin, slowly let yourself down to your starting position and repeat the exercise.

Leg Raise: Lie on your back with your legs straight in the air forming a 90- degree angle. Lower your legs downward, stopping a few inches from the ground. Pause, and return to your starting position. Keep your back flat on the floor the entire time.

Balance: Balance on one foot. Foot extended low in front of you. Foot extended low in back of you. Foot extended low to the side.

Jumping Jacks: Jump to a position with your legs spread wide and your hands touching overhead and then returning to a position with your feet together and arms at your sides. A more intense version is to bend down (over) and touch the floor in between each jump.

Shoulder Rolls: Place your arms at your side while standing at attention. Lift your shoulders into an "up" position and roll them forward while pulling into your chest.

Lunges: Stand straight with your legs shoulder width apart. Keep your hands at your side. Step forward with one leg, bending at your knee to lower your body. Move back into your starting position and repeat. Alternate between legs after performing a number of reps.

Heel Raises: Stand on the floor with your feet pointing forward and about one foot apart. Keep your knees straight, but do not lock them into place. Raise yourself up onto the balls of your feet and squeeze your calf muscle. Hold this position before releasing back into your starting position.

Chair Dips: Sit in a chair with your hands placed firmly on the arms of the chair. Extend your legs out so they are resting on your heels. Lift your bottom up from the chair by extending your arms straight up. Lower yourself down by bending your elbows into a 90-degree angle. Do not let your bottom touch the chair. Push back up and repeat the exercise.

Crisscross: Lie on your back with your shoulders 3-5 inches off the ground and your heels raised off the floor. Keep your mid and lower sections of your back flat on the floor and keep your abdominal muscles tight. Rest your arms next to you on the floor. Cross your left foot over the right foot. Without stopping, rotate your feet so the right is over your left foot. Continue this pattern without resting.

Scissors: Lie on your back with your shoulders 3-5 inches off the ground and your heels raised off the floor. Raise your legs 3-5 more inches higher while keeping your legs straight. Alternate between legs so you are creating a scissor motion with your legs going up and down opposite each other.

Floor Bridge: Lie down on your back with your knees bent, feet flat on the floor. Rest your arms at your sides, palms down. Draw your belly in and push through your heels to lift your pelvis off the floor. Slowly lower your hips and pelvis back to the floor.

Leg Crab Kick: Get into a crab walk position by lying on your back and extending your arms and your legs up so you are supporting yourself with your hands and feet. Once your bottom is in the air, kick out with your right leg. Bring the right leg back and kick out with your left leg. Alternate between legs.

Air Jump Rope: Jump up and down while moving your arms in a circular motion as if you were swinging a jump rope.

Chest Touch Pushups: Start in an elevated position with your arms holding you up. Keep your body straight, head facing forward. Lower yourself towards the ground with both arms. Once your chest touches the ground start pushing back up to your starting position, while touching the left side of your chest with your right hand. Once completed drop your right arm down to the ground so you are holding yourself up with both arms in your starting position. Repeat the exercise, this time touching the right side of your chest with your left arm. Alternate between left and right.

Plank: Lie face down while resting on your forearms with your feet together. Sweep the floor with your arms to separate your shoulders and tuck your chin, creating a straight line from the top of your head to your heels. Hold this position.

Side Step: Lunge out to your right. Back leg straight, bend the right knee. Slide back and bend the left knee and straighten the right leg. Turn and face the opposite direction and repeat.

Mountain Climbers: Start in your pushup position. Then lift one leg a few inches off the ground and pull it up towards your chest. Hold your knee tucked in for 2 seconds, then return to your start position. Alternate legs like you are climbing up a mountain.

Toe Taps: Start by standing with your two feet shoulder length apart with your back straight and your arms by your sides. While jumping straight up, bring one toe forward to the front and tap while alternating to the opposite foot. Go back and forth between your left and right foot. Find a rhythm and be careful not to lose your balance!

NUTRITION

Hey Parents!

A healthy diet and daily exercise will maximize the likelihood of your child growing up healthy and strong. Children are constantly growing and adding bone and muscle mass, so a balanced diet is very important to their overall health. Try to provide three nutritious meals a day that all include fruits and vegetables. Try to limit fast food and cook at home as often as you can. Not only is it better on your pocketbook, cooking at home is better for you and can be done together as a family. Everyone can help and it is more likely you will eat together as a family.

As a healthy eating goal, avoid food and drinks that are high in sugar as much as possible. Provide fresh fruits, vegetables, grains, lean meats, chicken, fish and low-fat dairy items as much as possible.

---

5 Steps to Improve Eating Habits

 Make fresh fruits and vegetables readily available

 Cook more at home, and sit down for dinner as a family.

 Limit sugary drinks, cereals and desserts

 Serve smaller portions

 Limit snacks to 1 or 2 daily

HEALTHY EATING POP QUIZ!

What does eating
healthy mean to <u>you</u>?

List your 3 favorite healthy foods:

1) _____   2) _____   3) _____

If you were only to eat vegetables,
what 5 vegetables would you choose?

1) _____   2) _____

3) _____   4) _____   5) _____

Fill in the names of 5 different food groups on the Food Plate.

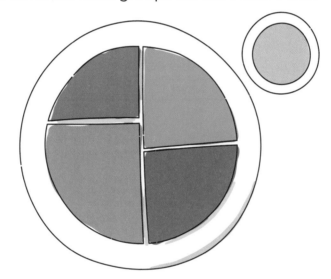

Circle the food and drink items that are healthy foods from the list below:

Milk	Apple	Chicken	Salad
candy	butter	soda	orange
ice cream	carrot	cotton candy	chocolate shake

List your 3 favorite healthy foods

1) _____   2) _____   3) _____

Create a list of foods you would like to grow in a garden

3-4 • © Summer Fit Activities™

Nutrition – *Food Plate*

It is important to eat different foods from the 5 different food groups. Eating a variety of foods helps you stay healthy. Some foods give you protein and fats. Other foods give you vitamins, minerals and carbohydrates. Your body needs all of these to grow healthy and strong!

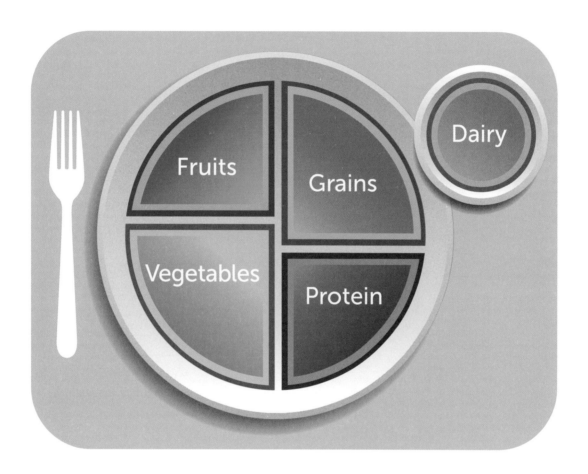

List 3 different foods for each category.

Fruits	Vegetables	Grains	Protein	Dairy
1) _____	1) _____	1) _____	1) _____	1) _____
2) _____	2) _____	2) _____	2) _____	2) _____
3) _____	3) _____	3) _____	3) _____	3) _____

Nutrition – *Meal Planner*

Plan out 3 balanced meals for one day.
Organize your meals so you will eat all the
recommended foods listed on the Food Plate.

BREAKFAST

LUNCH

DINNER

3-4 • © Summer Fit Activities™

Nutrition – *Meal Tracker*

Use these charts to list the different foods from the different food categories on My Plate that you eat each day.
Every day you mark each food category color in the vegetable!

	Grains	Dairy	Protein	Fruits	Vegetables	
Monday						
Tuesday						
Wednesday						
Thursday						
Friday						
Saturday						
Sunday						

	Grains	Dairy	Protein	Fruits	Vegetables	
Monday						
Tuesday						
Wednesday						
Thursday						
Friday						
Saturday						
Sunday						

MY OWN HEALTHY SNACKS

Frozen Banana Slices

Prep Time: 10 minutes
Freezer Time: 2 hours
Yield: 2 servings, Good for all ages!
Ingredients: 2 fresh bananas
Directions: Peel the bananas and cut them into 5-6 slices each. Place the banana slices on a plate and place in freezer for 2 hours. Enjoy your frozen banana snack on a hot summer day!

Yogurt Parfaits

Prep Time: 15 minutes
Cook Time: 0 minutes
Yield: 4 servings, Good for all ages!
Ingredients: 2 cups fresh fruit, at least 2 different kinds (can also be thawed fresh fruit)
1 cup low-fat plain or soy yogurt
4 TBSP 100% fruit spread
1 cup granola or dry cereal
Directions: Wash and cut fruit into small pieces. In a bowl, mix the yogurt and fruit spread together. Layer each of the four parfaits as follows: Fruit Yogurt Granola (repeat) Enjoy!

Frozen Grapes

Prep Time: 10 minutes
Freezer Time: 2 hours
Yield: 4 servings, Good for all ages!
Ingredients: Seedless grapes
Directions: Wash seedless grapes and separate them from their stem. Place into a bowl or plastic bag. Put them into the freezer for 2 hours. Enjoy your cold, sweet and crunchy treat!

Fruit Smoothies

Prep Time: 5 minutes
Cook Time: 0 minutes
Yield: 2 servings, Good for all ages!
Ingredients: 1 cup berries, fresh or frozen
4 ounces Greek yogurt
1/2 cup 100% apple juice
1 banana, cut into chunks
4 ice cubes
Directions: Place apple juice, yogurt, berries and banana into blender. Cover and blend until smooth. While the blender is running, drop ice cubes into the blender one at a time. Blend until smooth. Pour and enjoy!

3-4 • © Summer Fit Activities™

2
× 1
___

7

2
× 2
___

6

3
× 1
___

5

3
× 2
___

4

3
× 3
___

2

4
× 1
___

1

4
× 2
___

9

4
× 3
___

8

4
× 4
___

6

5
× 1
___

5

5
× 2
___

4

5
× 3
___

3

A

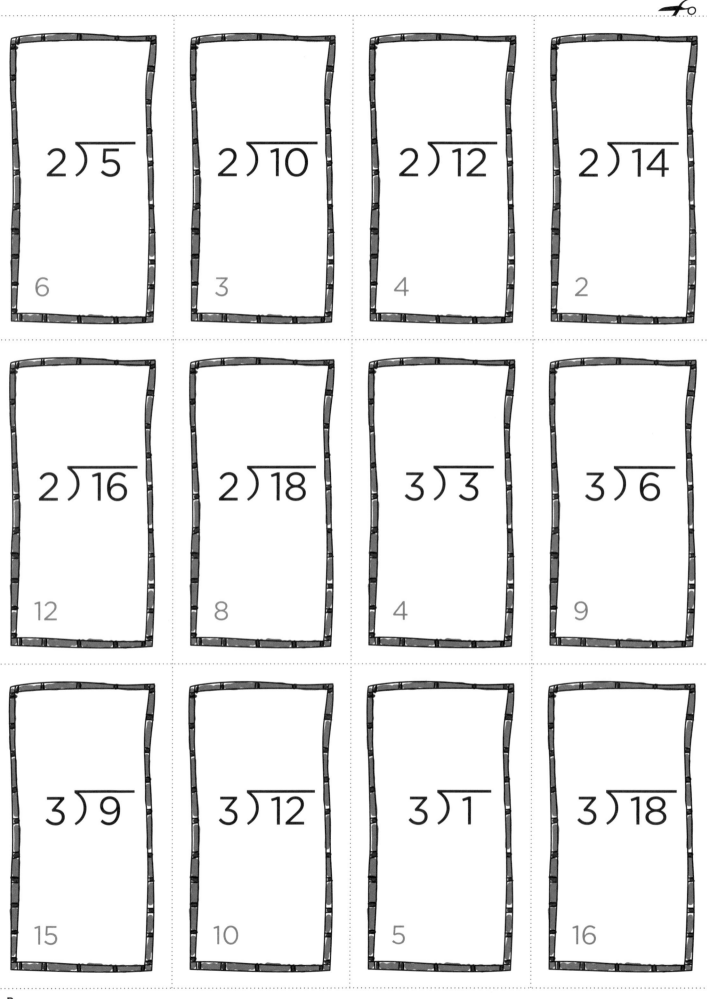

$2\overline{)5}$

6

$2\overline{)10}$

3

$2\overline{)12}$

4

$2\overline{)14}$

2

$2\overline{)16}$

12

$2\overline{)18}$

8

$3\overline{)3}$

4

$3\overline{)6}$

9

$3\overline{)9}$

15

$3\overline{)12}$

10

$3\overline{)1}$

5

$3\overline{)18}$

16

B

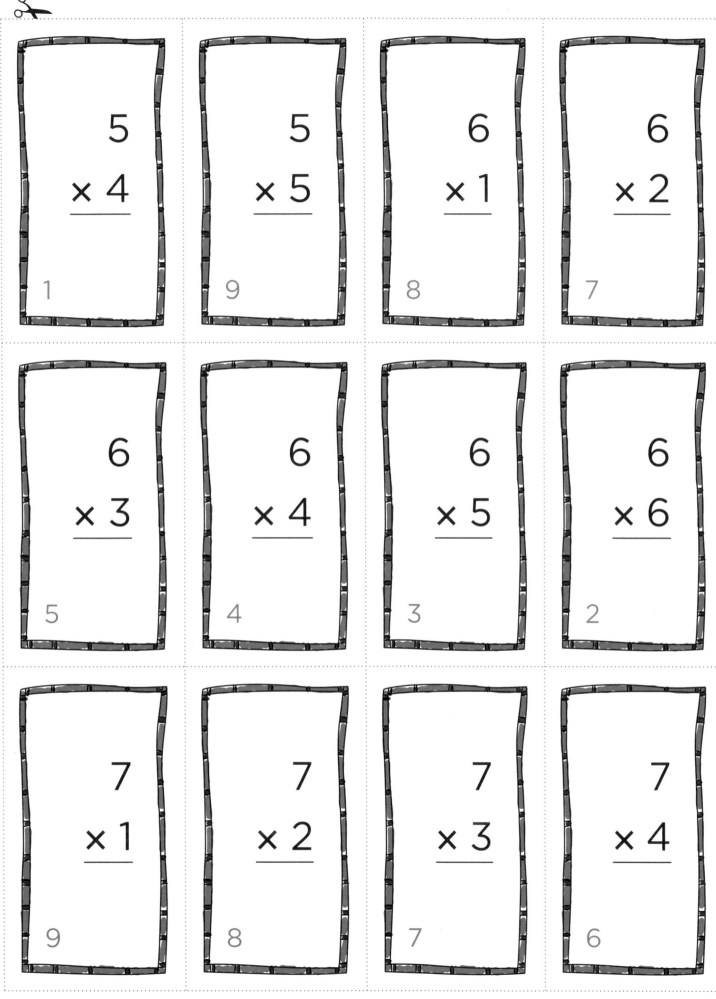

5
× 4

1

5
× 5

9

6
× 1

8

6
× 2

7

6
× 3

5

6
× 4

4

6
× 5

3

6
× 6

2

7
× 1

9

7
× 2

8

7
× 3

7

7
× 4

6

c

$3\overline{)21}$	$3\overline{)24}$	$3\overline{)27}$	$4\overline{)20}$
12	6	25	20
$4\overline{)8}$	$4\overline{)12}$	$4\overline{)16}$	$4\overline{)20}$
36	30	24	18
$4\overline{)24}$	$4\overline{)28}$	$4\overline{)32}$	$4\overline{)36}$
28	21	14	7

D

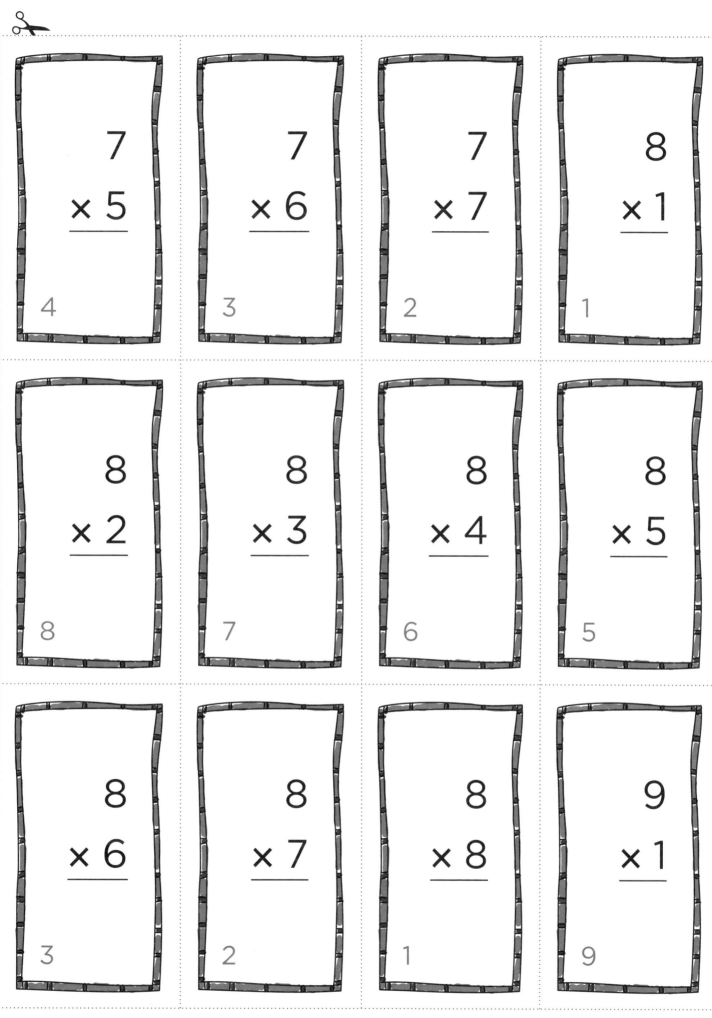

7
× 5
4

7
× 6
3

7
× 7
2

8
× 1
1

8
× 2
8

8
× 3
7

8
× 4
6

8
× 5
5

8
× 6
3

8
× 7
2

8
× 8
1

9
× 1
9

E

$5 \overline{)5}$

8

$5 \overline{)10}$

49

$5 \overline{)15}$

42

$5 \overline{)20}$

35

$5 \overline{)25}$

40

$5 \overline{)30}$

32

$5 \overline{)50}$

24

$5 \overline{)40}$

16

$6 \overline{)45}$

9

$6 \overline{)6}$

64

$6 \overline{)12}$

56

$6 \overline{)18}$

48

F

drink

eight

fall

far

clean

cut

done

draw

about

better

bring

carry

kind	hot	full
laugh	hurt	got
light	if	grow
long	keep	hold

H

show

six

small

start

own

pick

seven

shall

much

myself

never

only

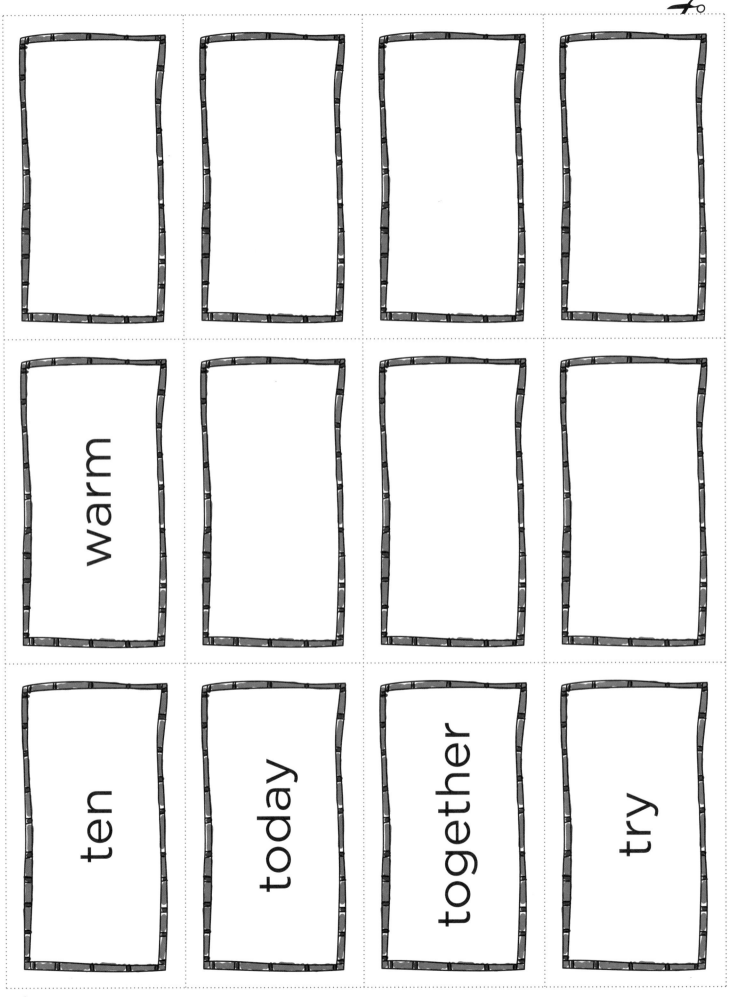

warm

ten

today

together

try

J

Value of **Curiosity**

Value of **Humor**

Value of **Love**

Value of **Kindness**

Value of **Dedication**

Value of **Friendship**

Value of **Giving**

Value of **Saving**

Value of **Understanding**

Value of **Imagination**

Value of **Responsibility**

Value of **Helping**

K

Desire to know or learn something

To be committed to a task or purpose

Aware of, and interested in learning other people, ideas and beliefs

Positive state of mind, being funny

Mutual trust and support between people

Ability to be creative and resourceful

Deep affection and caring for another person

To offer or hand over something

Being accountable for your actions and other peoples

Being friendly, generous, considerate

Preventing the waste of something

To contribute and offer assistance

L

Value of **Truth**

Value of **Belief**

Value of **Respect**

Value of **Courage**

Value of **Honesty**

Value of **Sharing**

Value of **Patience**

Value of **Determination**

Value of **Caring**

Value of **Foresight**

Value of **Learning**

Value of **Fantasy**

M

Ability to do
something that
frightens you

Admire someone
for their abilities,
qualities or
achievements

Trust, faith or
confidence in
someone or
something

A fact, belief or
person that is
accepted as
being true

Being resolute to an
idea or purpose

Accept or
tolerate without
getting upset

To give to others

Sincere, free
of deceit

Being able to
imagine the
impossible

Knowledge through
experience, study or
being taught

Being able to
predict needs or
what will happen in
the future

Displaying kindness
and concern
for others

CERTIFICATE OF COMPLETION

Summer Fit Activities

Has Completed

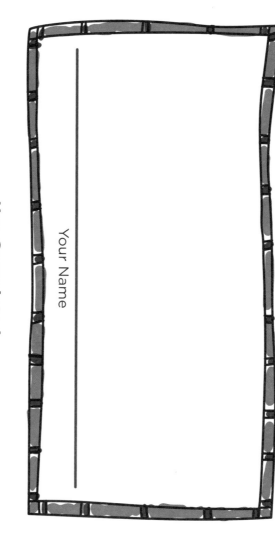

Your Name

Parent Signature

SummerFitActivities.com

P